*Collecting
Tomorrow's
Antiques
Today*

Collecting
Tomorrow's
Antiques
Today

NORMAN FLAYDERMAN
EDNA LAGERWALL

Garden City, New York
Doubleday & Company, Inc.
1972

ISBN: 0-385-06175-7
Library of Congress Catalog Card Number 71-186021
Copyright © 1972 by Norman Flayderman and Edna R. Lagerwall
Printed in the United States of America

FOREWORD

The twentieth century is certain to go down in the annals of history as one of the greatest, most exciting eras. By the reckoning of time there is still more than a quarter of a century to go before the year 2000 is ushered in. Considering the tremendous inventions and discoveries, innovations in styles and customs of this epoch, one cannot help but feel that the coming two decades will bring about even more stupendous contributions in achievements and progress.

Looking back to the beginning of the 1900s, none but scientists could foresee the things to come: electricity, the telephone, the automobile, refrigeration, sound pictures, radio, television, computers, air travel and space exploration. And little did anyone realize what significant industrial and sociological changes would evolve from woman suffrage, prohibition and its repeal, social security, labor unions and the emancipation of the worker, merely mentioning a few. To future historians, it will most certainly appear that we, "the twentieth-century people," contributed rapidly to the advancements of civilization.

Never before have there been such beautiful and exciting collectibles around us which for the discerning collectors open new avenues of adventure, knowledge and investment. In collecting tomorrow's antiques today, you will have the fun of looking ahead to the future and at the same time delving into the past. Success in this area does require, to a nominal degree, some knowledge of authentic antiques. It is important to know the objects of the past which have survived the years and become cherished heirlooms, and to recognize the names of firms which date back to colonial days and are still actively in existence. In evaluating antiques, as you will discover, age alone is not the determining factor. Rarity, inherent qualities of good taste, historic interest, beauty and craftsmanship are of the utmost significance. These same prerequisites apply to every phase of modern collecting.

It is encouraging to note the constantly growing interest in collecting modern pieces which has literally hit the country with all the excitement of the 1849 Gold Rush. This is quite understandable, for in the world of rare antiques there are fewer pieces available and the market is largely dominated by wealthy private collectors whose aims are either cultural or for investment as a hedge against inflation. Museums, too, are assembling fine collections either through purchases or gifts. Thus, when the demand becomes greater than the supply, prices soar and often are unaffordable to the average collector. Prices in every area of collecting, as you will learn, fluctuate in the same manner as the stock market, and vary from time to time and dealer to dealer.

Collecting, as a hobby or avocation, is a great source of pleasure to a multitude of people. Those of a visionary nature are turning to modern collectibles of which there is no scarcity. Limited editions, of course, are the most desirable and already the market on figural bottles, commemorative plates, medallic art, militaria and other items reflect the intense interest in the subject.

This seems essentially the time for modern collecting, particularly in view of these two exciting, promising and vital factors:

(1) The American Bicentennial (1776–1976) will be celebrated with patriotic vigor. Great new items, commemorating this occasion, are already being manufactured and in many instances advisability for advance orders publicized. If memorabilia of the past great world's fairs, expositions and momentous historic events have reached such consequential meaning in the collecting world, you can well imagine the future significance of American Bicentennial acquisitions. In addition to the nation, many individual states of the union are commemorating their own centennials around this period.

(2) Fabulous man-made materials, from plastics to nylons, have come into existence during the past several decades and many more are on the way. It is no idle supposition that startling new discoveries will result from our exploration of outer space.

In your own collecting, choose the field you enjoy and follow your own inclinations in judgment and taste. Remember, everything that is an antique today was new yesterday; and everything new today will be an antique tomorrow. Good luck!

NORMAN FLAYDERMAN
EDNA LAGERWALL

ACKNOWLEDGMENTS

We are deeply appreciative of the assistance, enthusiasm and encouragement which we received from collectors, manufacturers, dealers, editors, staff writers, authors and our publishers, Doubleday & Company, Inc.

M. Alber (David O. Alber Associates, Inc.); David Armstrong (Armstrong's).

E. Babka (the *Antique Trader Weekly*); Bee Baldwin (Tiffany & Company); William K. Bass (The Coca-Cola Company); Isabelle Bates (collector); Mary A. Benjamin (Walter R. Benjamin Autographs, Inc.); Jean Bennett (Doubleday & Company, Inc.); Fred Bertram (The Judaic Heritage Society); Dorothy Foster Brown (author).

Mark Carlton (Avon Bottle Collectors Club); Michael C. Cerullo, (International Mint); Kathryn Chumasero (collector); Clara Claasen (Doubleday & Company, Inc.); Alice Coester (collector); Claudia Coleman (Wedgwood); D. Stanley Corcoran (Corcoran Crystal); Marjorie Crodelle (Clark, Nelson, Ltd.); Jack Cumming (Mattel); Elsa Curry (collector).

Muiriel Davis (Joyce Memorial Library); Caroline Delfino (Royal Worcester Porcelain Co., Inc.); Lawrence R. Dorgin (Tudor House); Arthur Drapeau (collector).

Robert L. Edwards (Corning Glass Works); George Erfurt (Frankfort Distillers Company); Dona Everson (collector).

Milton Fenster Associates, Inc. (Public Relations); Heidi Fischer (Plummer-McCutcheon); Susan Flayderman (N. Flayderman & Company, Inc.); Rita Ford (Rita Ford, Inc.).

Frank Gavitt (Toy Manufacturers of America); Ashby Giles (F. A. O. Schwarz); Bruce Gimelson (Bernard and Bruce Gimelson, Inc.); F. H. Griffith (collector, editor); Dr. Clara R. Gross (collector).

Barbara Haley (International Avon Collectors Club); Charles Hamilton (Charles Hamilton Autographs Inc.); Frederick Haviland (Haviland & Co., Incorporated); Joyce Hermonat (collector).

Kathryn Intemann (Needham & Grohmann, Inc.); Kenneth Irsay (David O. Alber Associates, Inc.); Dr. Consuelo Ives (Currier & Ives Family).

Agnes B. Johnson (collector); D. Wayne Johnson (Medallic Art Company); Lyle R. Johnson (Chein Playthings); Paul Jokelson (Cristal d'Albret).

Angela Kaufman (Svend Jensen of Denmark, Inc.); Katherine C. Kennedy (collector); Lucile J. Kennedy (Imperial Glass Corporation); William F. Krieg (The Franklin Mint); Harold Kuebler (Doubleday & Company, Inc.); Even G. Kulsveen (Lionstone Distilleries, Ltd.); Richard Kuntzsch (Crest Studio); Wilbur G. Kurtz, Jr. (The Coca-Cola Company).

Latama Inc.; Isobel C. Lee (Steuben Glass); Howard Lesser (Old Charter-Dant Distillers Company); Martin Lewin (James B. Beam Distilling Co.); Cecilia Lewis (Milton Fenster Associates, Inc.); William Trees Louth (Medallic Art Company).

Richard E. Martin (Famous Firsts Ltd.); Ted Materna (Ted Materna Associates); E. Christian Mattson (antiques); Evelyn R. Maximon (Wedgwood Collectors Society); Mort Mazor (The Fleischmann Distilling Corporation); Thomas G. McCaskey (Colonial Williamsburg); Dr. Ellen McDevitt (collector); L. G. McGinnis (J. A. Buchroeder & Company, Inc.); Richard D. McNeill (Fisher, Bruce & Co.); John Mebane (*Antiques Journal*); Mike Moran (designer).

Robert C. Pearce (G. Schirmer, Inc.); L. Pennington (collector); Henry A. Pickard, Jr. (Pickard, Inc.); Emil S. Polk (Collectors International Limited) Dorothy Powills (*Hobbies* magazine & Chicago Playing Card Collectors' Inc.).

Lisa Ray (Doubleday & Company, Inc.); William B. Riordan (Baccarat Crystal); Rosenthal U.S.A. Ltd.; Julia Ruman (Hearst Publications).

Robert Schecter (Double Springs Distillers, Inc.); Dorothy Schling (Scott-Fanton Museum); Charles Schwartz (Chas. Schwartz & Son); M. Schwartz (Alexander Dolls Co., Inc.); L. H. Selman (L. H. Selman Antiques); Anita Sheldon (Ginori Fifth Avenue); Donald Smith (Abercrombie & Fitch Co.); Per Sorensen (A. Michelsen, Denmark); Claudette Sparandero (Spode Incorporated); Michael Spina (E. Martinoni Co.); C. F. Stevens (The United States Playing Card Company); Dolores Storzinger (Georg Jensen, Inc.); Sandy Stotts (Mattel); Lynn R. Stuart (author).

Mildred Terrill (Joyce Memorial Library); Joseph P. Tremont (Ezra Brooks Distilling Co.); Lois Tuck (Joyce Memorial Library); Tudor House.

André Vulliet (Baccarat Crystal).

J. Weiss (*Western Collector*); Irene Weissman (Roy Blumenthal International Associates, Inc.); Ronald Wellstood (collector).

Raymond Zrike (Royal Worcester Porcelain Co., Inc.).

CONTENTS

xiv   *Contents*

LIST OF ILLUSTRATIONS

CHAPTER I

PORCELAIN AND POTTERY

Porcelain and pottery are as different as day and night, yet virtually both come under the generic term of ceramics (Gr. *keramos,* potter's clay).

PORCELAIN

Porcelain is most often referred to as "china" after the country of its origin. Around the fourteenth century it was first brought sparingly into Europe from the Orient where the splendor of the potter's art had attained the highest perfection.

Whether fact or fiction, the story goes that porcelain derived its name from Marco Polo when he was traveling through China. Upon examining carefully the royal treasures of Kublai Khan, he considered the richly decorated, delicate and translucent bowls, plates, cups, vases and ewers as beautiful as the most precious jewels he had ever seen. Supposedly, he exclaimed, "Porcellana!", the Italian word for a white shell.

Specimens of rare, early Chinese porcelain are seldom seen today except in museums. Even if in abundance, comparatively few of the choice pieces would be within the price range of the average person. And, too, their possession would impose costly insurance, and most likely, if stolen, the services of a modern-day Sherlock Holmes.

Among the expert collectors there is a group of purists who are most insistent that porcelain be called "porcelain" and not "china" which they consider too much of a generic term. They have a point, to be sure, but Shakespeare was also speaking of porcelain in *Measure for Measure*, Act II, Scene I, when Claudio speaks to Escalus, ". . . they are not China dishes, but very good dishes."

From the early sixteenth century to the beginning of the eighteenth (especially in Italy and France), innumerable attempts were made to produce translucent porcelain comparable to that of the Chinese. Although it is recorded that successful translucent porcelain was made in Venice in the fifteenth century, there are no known specimens to verify this. The earliest existing Italian specimens are Medici porcelain, made in Florence for Francesco, grand duke of Tuscany, between 1575 and 1580. Very few pieces were made except for the ruler's own personal use and as gifts. They had the qualities of Chinese natural porcelain, but were very costly to produce, and manufacture ceased entirely after Francesco's death. Then, nearly a century passed before porcelain was made again in Europe.

Porcelain was regarded as an artificial substance; an unknown between pottery and glass. What the early porcelain makers did not discover, until after many years of trial and error, was the oriental secret of using kaolinic clay (the whitest clay known, derived from felspathic rocks such as granite) as the true material required for hard porcelain. Much of it existed throughout Europe, but Germany was the first country to discover it and in an accidental manner. Porcelain makers then took such great pride in the use of kaolinic clay that they stamped early pieces with the word, "Felspar."

From the first attempts the porcelain of Germany was of true kaolinic clay. It was purely a chance discovery by a young chemist, Frederick Boettger, in 1710. One day while dressing his wig he was impressed with the quality and whiteness of the new hair powder in vogue. When he learned that it was a finely powdered white clay, he decided to use it in ceramic ware, and thus discovered the true material for hard porcelain. When Augustus II, elector of Saxony, heard about this, he established a porcelain manufactory for initial experimentation at the Castle of Albrechtsburg in Meissen and then for manufacture at Dresden, a short distance away. Therefore, when you hear early Meissen and then Dresden, remember they are the one and same manufactory and the names are used interchangeably. The antique Meissen (Dresden) were copies from the Chinese; this was followed by elaborate decorations of flowers, or reproductions of oil paintings by Dutch and Flemish masters.

The beginning of porcelain manufacture in England is somewhat complicated and the earliest known specimens are from 1745 and bear the name "Chelsea." The Bow factory was probably in existence, but its porcelain has not been truly identified. Lowestoft and Bristol then followed. It is sufficient for a book of this nature to begin with Royal Crown Derby (1750) and Royal Worcester (1751) as both companies are in existence today and are producing exquisite work.

It was the success of the natural kaolinic porcelain produced in Germany and England which led to the manufactory of Sèvres in France under the reign of Louis XV. The king, like other leading rulers of the times, followed the fashion of establishing a royal manufactory of porcelain either to satisfy personal whims or for monetary gain. Sèvres is also in production today as well as Meissen (Dresden) which is behind the Iron Curtain and has limited exports.

America was content to import its porcelain until the nineteenth century, although, as we know, pottery was made from the days of the Indians. It is of interesting note, however, that one or two English porcelain makers attempted to make paste with the help of the American "unaker" or kaolinic clay found in this country.

Once you get the feeling of porcelain, you'll be able to recognize it quickly. It is delicate in appearance, and has a musical ring. If, by misfortune, a piece slips from your fingers on a deep, dense carpet, it may escape accidental damage and the strength and durability surprise you. Should it suffer by sad breakage, you will see strong, hard porcelain beneath the glaze. Please take our word for this, and be sure dropping a plate doesn't happen to you as it did to one of us—on a tile floor!

POTTERY

Pottery is synonymous with primitive ware and earthenware and the art of making it goes back to prehistoric days. At first the native clays were hardened by drying in the sun until it was discovered that fire-baked clay became as hard as stone. Among the fine varieties of glazed pottery are Majolica (Spanish); Delft (Dutch); Faïence (French); and Queen's Ware (English) which originally was called creamware by Josiah Wedgwood, but became Queen's Ware at the command of Queen Charlotte of England (wife of George III).

Before proceeding, the following definitions may be helpful to those who are not already familiar with the subject.

Ceramics, the art of modeling, molding and baking in clay. Derived from the Greek: *keramos,* potter's clay.

Pottery, or earthenware. A soft-paste ware made from local clays.

Porcelain, hard paste, containing the essential kaolinic clay.

Bone China, calcinized bone added to other ingredients and close to porcelain in appearance.

Bisque, unglazed porcelain.

Stoneware, hard paste ware with slight glaze; resembles porcelain.

Jasper Ware and Black Basalt, stoneware and two of the greatest achievements of Josiah Wedgwood.

Majolica, glazed pottery.

Faïence, glazed pottery.

Limoges, china-making center in France. Home of the famous Haviland manufactory, and it is well to remember that all Limoges is not Haviland.

Staffordshire, often confused as the name of a manufacturer. Staffordshire (between Liverpool and London) is a district in England referred to as the Potteries. Comprises the following towns and villages: Burslem, Cobridge, Etruria, Fenton, Hanley, Land End, Lane, Delph, Longton, Shelton, Stoke and Tunstall. As you may recall, Arnold Bennett immortalized five of these towns in his famous novel, *Anna of the Five Towns.* The original Staffordshire potters included Spode, Wedgwood, Minton and Clews.

There are literally dozens and dozens of porcelain and pottery manufacturers today. As a selective collector you must be careful to choose your pieces carefully. Our advice is: (1) Concentrate on the *limited editions,* as a mass-produced item deters the potential importance and value of a good collectible. (2) Search among the famous porcelain and pottery makers—Royal Crown Derby, Royal Worcester, Wedgwood, Spode, Haviland, Royal Copenhagen, Rosenthal, Royal Doulton, Bing & Grøndahl, Sèvres, Meissen (Dresden), Rörstrand, Lenox, etc. As the early creations of these manufacturers are now authentic antiques and command high prices, it is safe to surmise that new issues signed by them will have perpetually increasing worth. (3) Keep alert to the new manufacturers. Who knows which one is destined to become a future "Spode" or "Wedgwood?" (4) Do not completely shy away from the non-limited or mass-produced pieces. If you like something because you consider it beautiful, timely or original, purchase it. Porcelain and pottery are "perishables." There is a heavy attrition through breakage beyond repair and, too, many good pieces end up in the junk pile, never to be rescued even for a white elephant sale. This, of course, is all in favor of the collector—the fewer the pieces, the higher the potential value.

POTTER'S MARKS

To help you identify pieces, look for the potter's mark. Page 8 shows some of the more prevalent ones you will come across. Many you will recognize; others you will see for the first time.

Porcelain and pottery can be assembled in many forms. Now we will begin our happy collecting of figurines, commemorative plates, Toby jugs, Christmas plates, moon-landing plates, sculptured art and everything else we can think of in porcelain and pottery.

TOBY JUGS

The colorful Toby jug evolved from early drinking vessels, many of which were elaborately carved in wood or horns in a variety of fantastic forms and shapes including human faces. One of the earliest was the bellarmine,

COPELAND
SPODE
ENGLAND

PORSGRUND
P | P
NORWAY
54

M.J.Hümmel ®

WEDGWOOD
BONE CHINA
MADE IN
ENGLAND

Rörstrand

Rosenthal

®

ROYAL CROWN DERBY

51

ARABIA
MADE IN
FINLAND

ROYAL COPENHAGEN

 B&G   BING & GRØNDAHL.

PICKARD
CHINA
U.S.A.

ROYAL CROWN DERBY

HAVILAND
LIMOGES
FRANCE

a caricature of Cardinal Bellarmino, made for the Netherlands Protestants and dates back to the Middle Ages. A number of these were later found buried in cellars of Elizabethean homes, and this inspired the English potters to fashion their own versions of drinking jugs in human form. There are many stories of how the name, "Toby jug," originated. The one which we find most colorful is that the name was acquired from "my Uncle Toby" in Laurence Sterne's *Tristam Shandy*. A humorous drinking jug was made of his likeness which recalled how he smoked his pipe, drank his ale, told his tales and bellowed, "Our armies swore terribly in Flanders, but nothing to this."

Toby jugs are great collectors' items and, in general, appeal especially to men. Perhaps, as a collector told us, it's "because of the humor of the subjects and the association that they were first made to hold a draught of ale." Children find them amusing, especially the ones which portray famous men or characters they have read about in books. Usually Toby jugs are not meaningful nor dainty enough to please women, but are tolerated in a prized collection with a "peace at any price" attitude and a smug knowledge of knowing their worth. "They're devils to keep clean," a friend told us, "but, I get around it by telling my husband to do it himself as they are so valuable."

Spode, Rockingham, Copeland and all the other Staffordshire potters made Toby jugs and copies of the English jugs were made in America. The caricature idea became so popular that other eccentric and well-known characters were used for subjects. Large and small, you'll find Toby jugs depicting John Bull, Dickens' characters,

Falstaff, Lord Nelson, Winston Churchill, Franklin Roosevelt, innkeepers and sailors; and even a few women such as Sairey Gamp and Betsy Trotwood.

Nearly every known specimen of old Toby jugs is in the hands of collectors, and when you do find them on the dealer's market they run into extremely high prices. Interesting Toby jugs are being made today, but when they come out they are quickly snatched up, especially those which bear the mark of a famous maker.

Royal Doulton has a fine line including the "Figures and Character Jugs of Williamsburg" which we particularly like. For over two hundred years this famous manufactory has been known for its countless Toby jugs of fishermen, a fisherwoman, cobbler and his wife, cook and woodcutter—valuable collectors' pieces. Royal Doulton now perpetuates its old traditions with the figures and character jugs of Williamsburg. These jugs depict seven of Williamsburg's craftsmen—the Gaoler, Guardsman, Bootmaker, Blacksmith, Apothecary, Night Watchman and Gunsmith. They come in three sizes: large (height 7″), small (height 4″) and miniature (height 2½″). We feel that they belong in every Toby jug collection, and are of special importance and sentiment to those who have visited Colonial Williamsburg.

Beswick of England, who began making figures and Toby jugs in 1896, offers a good selection. They specialize in Dickens' characters, including Tony Weller, Martin Chuzzlewit and Little Nell's Grandfather. Although mass-produced they have good subject interest and will add to the enjoyment of any collection.

Real collecting of Toby jugs today belongs to those who are in earnest search, as relatively few are being made at present; but as time goes on even a "just for fun" collection may turn out to be lucrative.

CHRISTMAS PLATES

Beautiful Denmark, the land of romance and traditions, began the custom of issuing Christmas plates as far back as 1895. Sweden and Norway made Christmas plates in the early 1900s, discontinued and now have resumed with Germany, Holland, France and Spain following the mode with plates from their lands. Today collectors around the world are under the spell of collecting Christmas plates.

All collectors will enjoy *The Story of Royal Copenhagen Christmas Plates* and *The Story of Bing & Grøndahl Christmas Plates* by Pat Owen. They trace a delightful legend back to the days when the wealthy of Europe began the custom of giving their servants platters heaped with fruit, cakes, candies and other good things to eat at Christmastide. At first, the platters were of crude wood as the main purpose was the contents, hoping to bring a little cheer into the lives of the recipients with tasty treats to enjoy during the holiday season. The servants, naturally, looked forward each Christmas to receiving their gifts and since these people had few things in their homes which were not utilitarian, they began to decorate their walls with the platters after the food had been enjoyed. The platters then became of significant importance when it was discovered that the servants referred to them as their "Christmas plates." Porcelain makers memorialized the custom around the turn of the century, and its popularity increases with the years.

BING & GRØNDAHL: Founded in 1853, Bing & Grøndahl made its first Christmas plate in 1895. Five hundred were issued which makes it understandable why dealers will say, "Not available," when questioned by eager collectors. Occasionally, though, there is one on the market in the range of $500 to $1,900. Supply and demand dictate the prices, and it is well to keep abreast of what the various dealers around the country are asking by reading *Hobbies* magazine, the *Antique Trader Weekly* and other reliable collectors' publications. You will find a variance in prices as one dealer may be stocked with a certain issue, and then other dealers have none available. This contributes to the excitement of collecting.

Originally, the Bing & Grøndahl 1895 plate sold for around $5.00. These plates all measure 7" in diameter with the exception of the double-size Jubilee plates, issued every five years. The 1970 Jubilee Year plate retailed for $25. It is amazing how these plates increase in value. The 1940 is listed at $1,100 in a recent dealer's catalogue. The Bing & Grøndahl potter's mark on the back has always been three towers with B&G underneath.

ROYAL COPENHAGEN: In 1908 Royal Copenhagen (established in 1779) became Bing & Grøndahl's friendly competitor of Christmas plates. The success and popularity of the B&G issues showed that there was plenty of room in the European and American markets for both companies. If you have a Royal Copenhagen 1908, hang onto it (see Valuations in the Appendix), as it seems permanently on the "Not available" list of dealers. For easy identification Royal Copenhagen has a border (Bing & Grøndahl has no border), and a variety of designs was used until 1914 when it was decided to adopt a standard border of pine cones and a star. Royal Copenhagen plates measure 7″ in diameter with the exception of 1908, 1909 and 1910 which were 6″. The custom is that on Christmas Eve the mold of the plate is broken, never to be reproduced, and the newest plate is added to collectors' shelves all over the world. The potter's mark, credited to Queen Juliane Marie, has three blue wavy lines symbolizing the three Danish waterways: the Sound, the Great Belt and the Little Belt.

Beginning in 1967, mugs to match were made which were priced around $9.50 for the small and $25 for the large. The 1967 mug is already on the dealer's market at $60.

RÖRSTRAND (Sweden): founded in 1726, is the oldest porcelain manufactory in Scandinavia and issued Christmas plates from 1904 through 1926. In 1968 this tradition was resumed with a limited production for collectors. The first issue, Bringing Home the Tree, was recently priced by some dealers at $100. The 1969 issue was titled Jul and 1970, Nils with His Geese. The 1971 issue, Nils in Lapland, retailed around $10. Gunnar Nylund is the artist of this modern series.

PORSGRUND (Norway): This porcelain manufactory dates back to 1887 and its reputation is known throughout the world. In 1909 a limited edition Christmas plate was produced, and those few still in existence are in private collections and unattainable. In 1968 Porsgrund introduced a continuing series with their second plate, Church Scene, in a very limited quantity. Dealers have asked $35 for this, and approximately $15 for the 1969 Three Kings. The 1970 issue is titled Road to Bethlehem. The 1971 A Child is Born was issued at $8.00. There is a Porsgrund Jubilee plate in this series retailing at $22. For the first time in 1970 there was a matching mug at $12.50. As the years pass, a collection of Porsgrund Christmas plates should increase both in sentiment and value.

SVEND JENSEN (Denmark): The first issue of Christmas plates was 1970, Hans Christian Andersen's House and 1971, the Little Match Girl, both retailing at $15. These are unique as they tell the world about Denmark's wonderful storyteller, Hans Christian Andersen.

WEDGWOOD (England): Windsor Castle, 1969, was the date of the first issue and today on the dealer's market this plate is valued at three times its original price. Trafalgar Square, 1970, retailed for $25. Eight inches in diameter, it is typically Wedgwood—pale blue and white jasper, with the scene in the center in white bas-relief and a border of holly leaves around the plate. The 1971, Piccadilly Square, retailed at $30.

HAVILAND (France): Haviland collectors waited long and patiently for Christmas plates. In 1970 a series of original plates entitled the "Twelve Days of Christmas," was introduced by Haviland & Co., Incorporated (an American-based firm with manufacturing facilities in Limoges, France). The first issue was the Partridge in a Pear Tree and the second, 1971, Two Turtle Doves. Both retailed at $25, and there has already been an increase in value of the 1970 issue. The designer of the series is Remy

Hétreau, recognized in his native France not only as a fine illustrator, but also a successful painter and sculptor.

BAREUTHER (Bavaria): Winter scenes in the spirit of *Weinachten* (Christmas) have been issued in the Bareuther Christmas plates since 1967. Stifskirche, the first issue, has more than quadrupled in price (see Valuations in the Appendix).

SPODE (England): Lovers of Spode would have paid more than the retail price of $30 for the first Spode Christmas plate (partridge) issued in a strictly limited and unrepeatable number in 1970. Each year there will be another new and beautiful plate. The 1972 issue, at $35 retail, was inspired by a popular Christmas carol "Ding Dong! Merrily on High."

HUMMEL: The first Christmas plate was introduced in 1971 at $25.

There are other Christmas plates by Rosenthal, Royal Delft, Lund & Clausen, Marmot, Frankoma, Belleek and, of course, many in crystal which you will find under the chapter, "Glass."

The collecting of Christmas plates is extremely personal and diversified. Many collectors concentrate on the manufacturer with reasons such as: "If it's Haviland, I must have it," or "I prefer Wedgwood." Others place emphasis on attempting to collect every issue of the two oldest makers of Christmas plates—Bing & Grøndahl and Royal Copenhagen. Perhaps the largest group of collectors are those with sentimental feelings and you will hear them say, "My grandparents were born in Germany," or "The Christmas scenes are more spiritual." Decide for yourself what you will collect and you will be happy and should the time come when your collection no longer holds interest, remember there will always be a buyer. It's doubtful you will ever lose a penny, and more likely you will come out richer.

MUGS

The modern universal custom of the midmorning "coffee break," in practically every home and office, has brought the drinking vessel called the "mug" or "tankard" (with one handle) into the greatest popularity it has ever enjoyed.

Mugs are interesting collectors' items and during the past few years some very fascinating ones have been issued. Wedgwood, for example, produced an attractive commemorative mug on the occasion of the investiture of the Prince of Wales at Caernarvon in July 1969. Another Wedgwood for this same occasion reproduced an early print of Caernarvon Castle. These are real collectors' pieces and it is doubtful that many, if any, will be found on the American market.

Under our discussion of Christmas plates we have already mentioned the matching mugs issued by Porsgrund and Royal Copenhagen. The Royal Copenhagen mugs are prominently dated, modern in design and in the traditional cobalt blue and white. The first issue (1970) came out for $20 large and $9.00 small. Both have experienced dramatic increases in value.

There are mugs of every description including signs

of the zodiac, colleges, historic scenes, Currier & Ives, old cars, political, famous persons. These are all worth collecting.

And, along this line, gather together a few of the inexpensive mugs labeled: Maxwell House, Hills Bros., Sanka, Yuban, Campbell-up and Irish Coffee (same as used at Shannon Airport). These are mass-produced souvenir items and not well regarded either as good design or ceramic ware, but as most of them will be broken or thrown away, it is not likely many will be around in the future. Items of this nature are definitely twentieth century and worth considering, as who ever dreamed that the early Coca-Cola bottles would be fetching the enormous prices of today?

COMMEMORATIVE PLATES

During the early 1900s richly decorated table service became the fashion and great artists were given special commissions for delicately hand-painted plates and platters. In depicting palaces of the kings, important national scenes and great occasions honoring important people, these plates became known as commemorative pieces. Royal Worcester, Spode, Royal Doulton, Wedgwood and other fine porcelain manufactories quickly realized the appealing interest of these plates, and began to produce a variety for public offering. Examining the porcelain of the past, you will see beautiful commemorative plates; the picture has not lessened today as plates of this type are in great demand, and in issuing them hardly any subject has been neglected, from momentous events in history to the celebration and observance of Mother's Day and Father's Day which we will begin with:

MOTHER'S DAY: This day of the year, honoring Mother, has been in existence for a half century, but plates commemorating the occasion are comparatively recent. As you will note, the list of manufacturers is brief, but again, of those issued, a number have greatly increased in value over their retail prices which range from $7.50 to $15:

Bing & Grøndahl	1969	Dog and Puppies (1st issue)
	1970	Bird and Chicks
	1971	Cat and Kittens
Bareuther	1969	Mother and Children (1st issue)
	1970	Mother and Children
	1971	Mother and Children
Royal Copenhagen	1971	
Porsgrund	1970	Mare and Foal (1st issue)
	1971	Boy and Geese
Svend Jensen	1970	A Bouquet for Mother (1st issue)
	1971	Mother's Love
Lund & Clausen	1970	Rose (1st issue)
	1971	Forget-me-nots

There are other Mother's Day plates including Blue Delft, Berlin, Ellard, Stumar and a Spanish Mother's Day plate in the $10–$15 range.

FATHER'S DAY: We have heard that Father's Day was in existence long before Mother's Day. Most of the plates

were introduced in 1970 with the exception of a Bareuther Father's Day plate, Rhine Castle (first issue, 1969,
and the price has more than tripled from the original
$12). The first issues of Porsgrund and Svend Jensen are
1971.

A woman we know, who displays great talent in table
settings, has started a collection of Father's Day plates
by the various makers to use as service or dessert plates
on that big day every June. Sounds like a fine idea as
collector's items of a functional nature should be used
and enjoyed.

MOON PLATES: Now you are launched on a new, out-
of-this-world adventure in collecting commemorative
plates. Moon plates belong in every collection and there
are many beautiful ones on the market by famous manufacturers.

As a worthwhile addition to your collection, we suggest
that you purchase one of each of the following and you
will have a striking and valuable display.

> *Wedgwood*—Man on the Moon—Apollo Eleven is-
> sued at $30. (Remember what happened
> to the first Wedgwood Christmas plate
> and how after one year it jumped to
> double the original price.)
> *Royal Copenhagen*—Moon Landing (retailed at
> $17.50)
> *Bing & Grøndahl*—Moon Plate ($33)
> *Lund & Clausen*—Moon Landing ($13)
> *Royal Delft*—Apollo 8 ($27.50) and Apollo 11 ($30)

It isn't too difficult to guess what astronomical worth these plates will have in years to come. Keep your eyes open for every new space plate issued. We've heard that many parents, relatives and friends of a child born on July 20, 1969, have purchased the Apollo 11 plate to serve the dual purpose of the birth date and the landing on the moon.

HAVILAND PRESIDENTIAL CHINA: Haviland & Co., Incorporated has introduced a series of four beautiful presidential plates. Each is a replica of the originals of the dinnerware which Haviland made for the White House. The originals are so extremely rare that most of them can only be seen in the White House China Room, or at the Smithsonian Institution. These new editions are limited to 2,500–3,000. Positively no additional reissues will ever be made.

The first four plates are:

> Martha Washington plate
> Abraham Lincoln commemorative
> Ulysses S. Grant commemorative
> Rutherford B. Hayes commemorative

The original retail price for each was around $100. Reports have come in that the Lincoln plate has already commanded as high as $600.

These new Haviland commemoratives are inscribed and signed by Theodore Haviland 2nd, the present president of the firm. As an illustration, the President Grant plate reads: "Authentic reproduction of a plate of White House China made by Haviland at Limoges, France, for

President Ulysses S. Grant and delivered on February 10, 1870. Limoges February 10, 1970. Theodore Haviland 2nd."

There will be little or no disappointment in collecting these plates, if you will order them from your store, or keep your local dealer aware of your interest.

WILLIAMSBURG COMMEMORATIVE PLATES BY WEDGWOOD: In lovely Wedgwood Queen's Ware, the Williamsburg commemorative plates follow the long-established American tradition of recording historic events and places on fine ceramic ware.

The set of twelve plates include: The Magazine, The Public Gaol, The Raleigh Tavern, The Court House of 1770, The St. George Tucker House, The George Wythe House, The Wren Building, The Quarter, The Capitol, The Governor's Palace, Bruton Paris Church and Archibald Blair's Storehouse. The distinguished American artist, Samuel Chamberlain, created the designs, and on the back of each plate is his signature, as well as a description of the center scene. Wedgwood in making these plates follows the old methods of transferring the designs from hand-engraved copperplates and firing them under the glaze. The complete set of twelve is less than $50 retail.

These are mass-produced, but we do not feel in so large a quantity as to distract from their appeal to collectors. We must remind you again that the factor of attrition will be in your favor as time goes on. These commemorative plates have three great attractions—the names of Wedgwood, Samuel Chamberlain and Colonial Williamsburg.

PLATES AD INFINITUM: Collectors of commemorative plates are most zealous in searching for the new and unusual, and the leading manufacturers are more than willing to please.

Here is a list of interesting pieces which we feel are definitely worth considering:

>*Royal Copenhagen Church Plates* (first five in a series of ten)
>>Roskilde Cathedral
>>Arhus
>>Ribe
>>Odense
>>Haderslev
>*Israel Commemorative Plates*
>>1967—Wailing Wall (1st issue)
>>1967—Tower of David
>>1968—Masada
>>1969—Rachel's Tomb
>>1970—Tiberias
>*Royal Copenhagen Commemorative Plate*
>>To celebrate the 750th anniversary of the "Dannebrog" (Danish flag)
>*Marmot President Plates*
>>George Washington (1st issue)
>*Wedgwood Calendar Plate*
>>1971 (1st issue)
>*Porsgrund Castle Plate*
>>1970 Hamlet's Castle (1st issue)
>*Schumann of Bavaria*
>>Composers plate—Beethoven—1970 (1st issue)

Wedgwood Mayflower Plate
>   1620–1970 (1st and only issue, 1970)

Lenox
>   Edward Boehm's works (very limited editions)

Pickard
>   Game Bird plates

Spode
>   Annual plates (1st issue, 1970)

Wedgwood
>   Wild Life plates

Our story of commemorative plates continues under the chapter, "Glass."

FIGURINES AND SCULPTURED ART

There is no beginning or ending to collecting in this field. It is a form of expression which has always come naturally to the talented artist; from the crudest primitive pottery pieces to beautiful *objets d'art*. In this category there are interesting pieces in every form to enjoy in our homes and offices.

Collecting figurines is within the realm of everyone from the small child with his inexpensive, supermarket ceramic figures of fairy-tale characters; the young couple who collects porcelain dogs and horses; to the wealthy connoisseur with every world auction gallery alerted to his desire for a very special and rare Dorothy Doughty bird.

There is hardly a home that does not have a figurine of one kind or another which is greatly cherished. Psychiatrists may tell us that figurines are the adults' playthings, but isn't it pleasant that we have them around to admire when "the world is too much with us?"

Perhaps it would be more enjoyable and helpful to you if we presented this subject in a categorical manner:

I. PEOPLE (Imaginary and Real): Haviland offers perfect renditions of the original sculptures by Jean Jacques Prolongeau, famous French sculptor, in the Little Princess; Peace, Prosperity; Mother and Child and the Fruit Bearer (each in the $20–$25 range). His Christmas sculptured series begins with the Dancing Angels (1971) and Prancing Horse (1972). These have been selected by us (we presume in the manner of Haviland) because of the artist's reputation. M. Prolongeau, who works in pottery stoneware, received wide acclaim in Tokyo in 1960 under the sponsorship of l'École de Paris—Arts Décoratifs. In 1963 he was granted the honor of presenting pieces of his ceramic art to the National Museum of Sèvres where a number of them have become part of the permanent collection.

If you are guided in this manner by both the reputation of the manufactory and the artist creating the work, you most certainly will assemble objects of beauty, importance and value. Frederick Gertner's "Historical Figures" series in Royal Worcester porcelain are beautiful, costly and in their own right antiques today, circa 1917. However, Neal French follows in Mr. Gertner's footsteps in the ambitious task of modeling a series of statuettes for Royal Worcester. He has a "Papal Figures" series (limited edition) which was exhibited in the Vatican Pavilion at the New York World's Fair in 1965. Another Royal Worcester series to consider is the "Military Commanders" series (limited edition) by Bernard Winskill, a sculptor of renown who has exhibited widely at the Royal Institute Gallery, the Society of Portrait Painters, the Paris Summer Salon and the Royal Glasgow Fine Arts Society. The first of the series is Napoleon Bonaparte, issued in 1969 in celebration of Bonaparte's birthday which was exactly 200 years previous. The price—$2,250. Now, especially in Royal Worcester, for the ladies are Freda Doughty's (sister of Dorothy Doughty) "Days of the Week," the enchanting nursery rhymes which begin with Monday's child and continue to the Child who is born on the Sabbath Day. These retail today between $40–$60 each and we have a friend who purchased hers through the years for around $15 or $20 each in America, but lower on her visits to Canada. They have been available for a considerable time and are a perennial favorite. However, we don't feel that the market is flooded as they are exquisitely fragile and the breakage is great since the majority of people regard small pieces (porcelain or pottery) simply as something beautiful without realizing their artistic quality and value to collectors. Along the lines of "Days of the Week" Royal Worcester also has a "Months of the Year" series.

Royal Worcester's "Victorian Figures" series (limited editions) by Ruth Van Ruyckevelt (wife of Ronald Van Ruyckevelt, known for his series, "American Game Birds," "Tropical Fish" and "Tropical Flowers") may, just possibly, turn into another great success such as this company achieved with the famous Dorothy Doughty birds. The subjects: the Tea Party, Charlotte and Jane, Bridget, etc., proved to be a particularly happy choice for her and she has handled it with fluency and delicacy. The editions are limited; no more than five hundred, and we have seen dealer prices listed as high as $1,500 for the Tea Party. The years of her work include 1964 to 1969, and at the present time, we presume, she is finishing her latest creations or engaged in research. Like every other Royal Worcester artist, Ruth Van Ruyckevelt is most precise and meticulous. Before attempting this ambitious series, she studied the fine collection of Victorian costumes in the Victoria and Albert Museum down to the most minute details of fitted sleeves, small turbans and flowerpot-shaped hats and the inevitable walking parasol which was fashionable with ladies who strolled along the smart West End of London. It has been said that Tissot's paintings gave her perceptive insight into this period.

Royal Doulton has produced many fascinating figurines in recent years including the famous two old peddlers, Balloon Man and Balloon Woman. People also collect Royal Doulton because the figurines are magnificent portrayals. Take a look at Lady Charman; Top o' the Hill and Darling (some say named by Queen Mary, who took a great fancy to this piece), and you will agree that they are good collectibles.

"Chelsea Figures" by Spode are a limited edition from the original molds, exactly as first produced in England in the 1700s. These delightful "little people" are retiring and no more will be made. For $125 (more or less) you can obtain the Huntsman (gentleman holding a wild fowl accompanied by a dog), Mistress Vernon (lady carrying a basket of fruit); and their friends: Gentleman Ranelagh, Lady Ranelagh, the Fruit Seller and Mistress Philoppots.

Now we come to everybody's love—Hummel. As we all

know, the imaginative artist who created these delightful, quiet and well-behaved children was Berta Hummel, a
Franciscan nun, known in her order as Sister Maria In-
nocentia (1934). The exclusive rights for making figurines
from her original drawings were granted to W. Goebel-
Porzellanfabrik whose traditions of porcelain making are
now in the fifth generation.

Hummel figurines are genuine collector's items and a
family tradition. Two or more members of the same household may each have his own collection as there have been
more than 280 Hummel figurines issued, but new issues
are not introduced frequently. In fact, the last time we
heard that W. Goebel introduced a new figurine from the
Berta Hummel sketches was for the opening of the "Hummel" Pavilion at the last New York World's Fair (1964–
65). (Hummel Christmas plates were issued in 1971.)

We want to stress that genuine Hummel figurines are
signed. They carry the M. I. Hummel signature indented
in the base together with the familiar "V" and "Bee"
trademark of W. Goebel-Porzellanfabrik; the only firm
authorized to make Hummel figurines. Collect Hummel,
by all means, and don't worry about how many are
around today; remember attrition will change the picture
tomorrow.

The "Beatrix Potter" series by Beswick of England is
doing extremely well these days. We confess that we have
been enchanted from childhood with Peter Rabbit, Tailor
of Gloucester, Old Woman in a Shoe and the others. Now
that they have been translated with extraordinary fidelity
by England's Royal Ballet in the MGM film, *The Tales of
Beatrix Potter*, we won't need to explain our "hang-up."
If you feel they are on the voluminous side of production,

again remember *attrition*. Beswick of England is an old firm, and at this writing (gossip) there has been a marriage to Royal Doulton. Less than $10 each, these figurines will give you enjoyment, and perhaps a future surprise in value.

II. ANIMALS, BIRDS, FISH, FLOWERS: This is art sculpture. We wish to guide you on the most selective pieces, in our estimation:

Doris Lindner who began her porcelain sculptures for Royal Worcester in 1931 with Fox and Hound has continued with her "Equestrian" series including Hog Hunting, Huntsman and Hounds, Cantering to the Post and Polo Player, which were priced around $350, circa 1936. In 1947 the queen of England requested Miss Lindner to model Princess Elizabeth (now Queen Elizabeth II) in the uniform of the colonel-in-chief of the Grenadier Guards riding "Tommy" (one of the Princess's favorite horses about whom we have read many stories). This was a very special assignment and, naturally, a most limited edition. However, it set a new style and scale for Miss Lindner's work which she has maintained ever since. For the three pieces of her most recent work: the "Prize Cattle" series: Dairy Shorthorn Bull (1966), Brahman Bull (1968) and Charolais Bull (1968), she traveled widely to gather material on champion cattle in Texas, to Canada to collect information for her model of a Royal Canadian Mounted Police, and to France to model Charolais Bull issued at $550.

Limited editions of five hundred are the "Game Bird" series, by Royal Worcester, and modeled by Ronald Van Ruyckevelt. Hunting in this field includes the Ring-

Necked Pheasant, Mallard Duck, American Woodcock, Green-Winged Teal, Bob White Quail and other feathered friends. Pricewise they are on the expensive side—Mallard Ducks and Ring-Necked Pheasants, $2,500 a pair. Essentially they are in the class of the Doughty birds which have been auctioned for as high as $36,000 for a pair of out-of-edition Quail. Her work is in major museums and private collections throughout the world. However, it is not improbable that you will find a Doughty bird at auctions, flea markets and in your own attic. Many have gone to nest in unlikely places and show up unexpectedly. If you see the Gray Wagtail ($750 current price) or Moorhen Chick (500 edition, with 73 completed), buy them, as you should expect appreciation in monetary value.

Also keep your eyes wide open for *The American Birds of Dorothy Doughty* which was published in 1962 by the Worcester Royal Porcelain Company Limited in Worcester, England. This is a fabulous book with handsome color plates of the American series of Doughty birds, vivid descriptions by Miss Doughty herself, and a critical appreciation by George Savage. It was published in a limited edition of 1,500 and originally sold for $65. We consider this a great collector's item in itself, and Raymond Zrike, president of Royal Worcester, told us that copies of this book sell as high as $1,000 today.

Cybis Porcelain, known throughout the world and acquired by art galleries and museums, is a collector's prize and as of now a good investment. According to a specialist in the field, "Closed limited editions have appreciated to many times the original cost." These pieces run the scale from low to high: Buffalo, $45; Squirrel, Mr. Fluffy Tail, $90; Colts, Darby and Joan, $250. Don't despair, there is a bunny, Mr. Snowball, at $20. Cybis is something to watch today.

The sculptures of Maurice Legendre were molded by Haviland, in limited editions, numbered and signed by the artist. The Fish, $300, The Bull, $200 and The Goat, $225.

Laszlo Ispanky (Ispanky Porcelain, Ltd., founded 1966) is known for his creative freedom and has to his honor sculptures in leading museums and galleries, and in offices and homes throughout the world. The American Collection, limited editions, includes:

Owl	$600.00
Drummer Boy	800.00
Horse	200.00
Unlimited Editions:	
Picnic	65.00
Susie	50.00
Huck Finn	100.00

The birds of Burgues are exquisite, inspired pieces. They emanate from the artist's studio at a high price, but if you will follow the collectors' publications you will ascertain the reasons.

The world of figurines and sculptured art is endless, and if we continued our research along these lines, we would never progress with this book. Porcelain and pottery are fabulous studies.

EPILOGUE:

If you are a beginner in this field:

(1) Concentrate on a specific manufacturer or artist.

1. President Hayes White House China, "Canvasback Duck" plate reissued by Haviland.

2. The unique feature of the Hayes Plate is the appearance of the Presidential Seal on the back rather than the front.

3. Wedgwood Zodiac Plate, courtesy of the Wedgwood Collectors Society.

4. Wedgwood Calendar Plate, courtesy Wedgewood.

5. Lockhart Bird Plates by Pickard, Inc., photo by Gibbs Studio.

6. Federal City Plates by Wedgwood, courtesy Chas. Schwartz & Son.

7. Wedgwood Safari Scenes, courtesy Wedgwood.

8. Harry Truman Commemorative Plate by Pickard, Inc.

9. Royal Copenhagen Moon Plate, courtesy Georg Jensen, Inc.

10. Wedgwood Apollo Plate, courtesy Wedgwood.

11. Holiday Plates Series, courtesy *the Antique Trader Weekly*.

12. Father's Day Plate 1971 by
Svend Jensen of Denmark, Inc.

13. Mother's Day Plate 1971 by
Svend Jensen of Denmark, Inc.

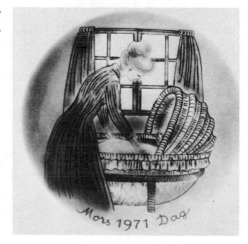

14. Porsgrund Mother's Day 1970
Plate, courtesy Fisher Bruce & Co.

15. Porsgrund Father's Day 1970 Plate, courtesy Fisher Bruce & Co.

16. Norman Rockwell Plate 1970 by The Franklin Mint.

17. Norman Rockwell Plate 1971 by The Franklin Mint.

18. Porsgrund Christmas Plate 1968, courtesy Fisher Bruce & Co.

19. Wedgwood Christmas Plate 1969, courtesy Wedgwood

20. Royal Copenhagen 1970 Christmas Plate, courtesy Georg Jensen, Inc.

21. 1971 Christmas Plate
by Svend Jensen of Denmark.

22. Bing & Grøndahl 1971
Christmas Plate, courtesy
D. Stanley Corcoran, Inc.

23. 1971 Plate in
"The Twelve Days of Christmas"
series by Haviland.

(2) Select a favorite subject: horses, dogs, cats, birds, children, etc.

Otherwise you will become bewildered and end up with a meaningless hodgepodge. The experienced collector needs no advice, but we hope that he, too, may glean a few interesting facts.

CHAPTER II

COMMEMORATIVE SPOONS

Spoon collecting is much in vogue. Apparently it has been for a long time, judging by the number of spoon collectors who form their own clubs for buying, selling and trading. It is a fascinating hobby, reasonably instructive and the cost within the reach of everyone.

Spoons come in several different sizes from the small four-inch demitasse, most prevalent in the commemorative line, to teaspoon and serving spoon dimensions. Their use ranges from soup to nuts: grapefruit, dessert, soda, salt, sugar, mustard, and the not-to-be-forgotten baby spoon which practically every infant receives (maybe a dozen or more, if he was born with a "silver spoon" in his mouth).

The collector's choice is endless with spoons commemorating countries, states, cities; presidents, rulers and other notables; fairs and expositions; historic events, centennials, colleges, famous landmarks and buildings; Christmas, Mother's Day and now, the Moon Landing. Signs of the zodiac, which began with Gorham in 1894, is an extremely popular issue today, with the current interest in astrology flourishing from coast to coast and around the world.

Spoons are of gold, sterling silver and silverplate, and many have handsomely enameled handles. Prices are from around a dollar up to twenty-five dollars or higher. Values usually increase with time, but not on a grand scale. In order to give you an idea of what old spoons are selling for today, we have studied dealers' listings. The following were probably purchased for around one dollar to five dollars, and in parentheses are recent market prices: Salem Witch spoon ($20); Washington Irving (Gorham; $22); Philadelphia spoon ($25); Bunker Hill —1775 ($10); St. Louis ($19); Actor's Fund Fair ($75, if and when available).

Commemorative spoons are on sale everywhere. You will find them in gift shops, department stores and wherever souvenirs are sold. And, too, browse through the shopping columns of magazines and you will be able to collect very fine and interesting spoons through mail order.

Many people become interested in collecting spoons after they discover a few real old ones at home which belonged to their mother or grandmother. Others become spoon collectors by accident or fate. This was the case of a woman physician we know who fell heiress to an interesting collection of approximately three hundred historical and commemorative spoons. Many were displayed on spoon racks, tarnish and all, and others in felt cases.

The doctor's first impulse was to give away what she called, "this junk." Fortunately, though, she showed the spoons to a friend who is interested in antiques. The woman polished the spoons and, in turn, brought them to a friend of hers who is a dealer.

"A nice collection," the man said, "and, it begins almost at the beginning." Examining them carefully, he then added, "I was hoping that there would be the 1881 Niagara Falls Suspension Bridge spoon which was the first of the souvenir and commemorative spoons and started the craze of manufacturing them. The fad died down, but is in full bloom again." Needless to say, upon realizing the beauty and value of the spoons, our friend kept the collection. It has been catalogued and she is now purchasing new issues relating to the subjects of special interest, especially the moon landing commemoratives.

If you are just beginning your collection, we highly recommend the beautiful Danish spoons by A. Michelsen, famous silversmiths founded in 1841 (Copenhagen) and selected by the king of Denmark as "Insignia Jewelers" in 1846. Since that year, A. Michelsen has been entrusted with the manufacture of decorations used by the royal house. Four generations of this family have headed the firm and Jorgen Michelsen is now chairman of the board. Their first souvenir spoon was designed in 1898 to commemorate the occasion of King Christian IX's eightieth birthday. The idea was novel and the workmanship so exquisite that souvenir spoons came into great demand and people waited patiently for each new Michelsen creation to appear. In 1910 their first Christmas spoon made its appearance, and up to now no year has ever passed without a new issue. The old spoons, 1910–39, are most difficult to obtain, even through dealers; but according to Mr. Per Sorensen, export manager of the firm, the issues from 1940 up to the present are still available from the workshop. However, it is the intention little by little to discontinue old issues and concentrate exclusively on making the Spoon of the Year (with matching fork). You can, now, readily see what great collector's items they are.

Recent *Christmas spoons:*

 1967: Splendor of Yule
    Design: Paul René Gauguin
    (grandson of the great French painter)
 1968: A Mother's Heart
    Design: Henry Heerup
 1969: Greenlander
    Design: Ib Antoni
 1970: Mr. Snowman's Christmas Tree
    Design: Mogens Zieler
 1971: Golden Universe
    Else Alfelt
    (Retail for $25)

Michelsen spoons measure approximately 6½ inches in length (larger than the average American teaspoon). They are made of fine sterling silver, gold-plated with multicolored-enamel embossing. We have been told that twenty-eight separate operations go into the making of one Christmas spoon. The artists are carefully chosen and work closely with the craftsmen, and the results are, as you will observe, an excellence of artistic beauty, sensitive quality of craftsmanship and timeless in good taste.

We discovered an interesting article on the Michelsen Company which appeared in the 1960 *Christmas, An American Annual of Christmas Literature and Art,* Volume 30, edited by Randolph E. Haugan (Augsburg Publishing House, Minneapolis, Minnesota). The publisher just might have a copy of this issue available, if you wish to write for it.

A. Michelsen has added a new collector's item to its exclusive line of silverware: twelve "Spoons of the Month." The spoons, modern in design, but in the best tradition of ancient Danish handicrafts, are made of sterling silver, enameled by hand, stamped with the Michelsen hallmark, artist's signature and the number of the month. They have been designed by Paul René Gauguin with corresponding symbols: gems, flowers, zodiac signs and astrological colors. Limited editions retail around $24. Among the fine shops selling these spoons are Danish Silversmiths, Inc. (New York).

From Holland there are Moon Landing spoons—commemorating Apollos 8 and 11, and we are certain others will follow. These retail for around $3.00 and belong in every collection. Other Dutch treats are: blue delft Christmas spoons (1970 and 1971); blue delft Father's Day spoon (1971); blue delft Mother's Day spoon (1971) —each in the neighborhood of $6.00.

Civil War buffs will like the Civil War Centennial spoons, hand-painted in colors on porcelain and a creation of the late Albert H. Oechsle. Thirteen for CWC (Confederacy) and nine for CWU (Union)—$6 each (or all twenty-two for $120).

Spoons will, undoubtedly, be appearing shortly in honor

of the American Bicentennial (1776–1976), and these will be collectors' finds, we feel certain.

Commemorative spoons are as functional as they are decorative. They make excellent conversation pieces with the serving of demitasse. And, if you enjoy your soft-cooked eggs in the shell, continental style, it is correct to use a spoon with a small bowl.

It is interesting to note the number of people who record their travels with a collection of commemorative spoons from the places they have visited. Unlike porcelain, pottery and glass, spoons take up practically no room, and best of all they are unbreakable (except for the very few in porcelain). Spoon collections add to the decor of a room when displayed on racks, tables or in smart glass cases. Even if you are not a collector, perhaps you have a friend who is. There is nothing more flattering to a hobbyist than to be remembered on birthdays, Christmas and other occasions with a piece to add to a treasured collection.

We haven't come across too many books on the subject of souvenir and historical spoons. An excellent, definitive reference is *American Spoons, Souvenir and Historical* by Dorothy T. Rainwater and Donna H. Felger (Thomas Nelson, Inc.). There are three books by Anton Hardt: *Souvenir Spoons of the 90's, Adventuring Further in Souvenir Spoons* and *A Third Harvest of Souvenir Spoons*. An out-of-print and rare book is: *The American Story of Spoons* by Albert Stutzenberger and you might look for a copy in your library.

Take our advice, "count your spoons," and watch your collection grow!

CHAPTER III

PAPERWEIGHTS

You are in the company of gem collectors when your interests turn to paperweights. The early, rare ones seldom are seen except in museums, on tours of historic houses and grand palaces, or in the homes of the wealthy. Sparkling with color and dazzling beauty, they are masterpieces in design and reflect the utmost talents of artisans whose medium is glass.

The idea of the glass paperweight originated in Venice, but the decorative features were of Egyptian origin. Although the art of paperweight making is ancient, it has been reputed that the first recorded specimen is Venetian, created by Pierre Bigaglia and dated 1845. The craft soon spread to France where Baccarat, St. Louis and Clichy, three famous glassmakers, produced them as a sideline. These names are known to every serious collector. Today Baccarat continues to make paperweights with St. Louis returning now and then with new releases, and Clichy is out of the picture completely. French paperweights were copied widely in England in the glassmaking centers of Bristol and Stourbridge. In America the successful import of French paperweights led to imitation in glass factories, and then to original creations.

Paperweights are a fascinating, but complex study. If you are a neophyte, begin by reading as much about them as you can. Three especially good books are: *Old Glass Paperweights* by E. H. Bergstrom; *Paperweights and other Glass Curiosities* by E. M. Elville; and *Sulphides: The Art of Cameo Incrustation* by Paul Jokelson.

It is not within the scope of this book to go into the technicalities of how paperweights are made, but we would like to familiarize you with a few of the varieties: millefiori (thousands of flowers—mosaic glass), sulphides or cameo incrustations* (heads of famous persons, mythological figures, historical events), magnums, miniatures, flowers and rare subjects (caterpillar, snake, duck, strawberry). In addition to the regular paperweights (cased glass) are the overlays. These are several layers of glass of different colors with designs cut through to show body color.

Paperweights were extremely popular in Victorian days and the ones which cost a pittance are now worth hundreds of dollars. As the very rare paperweights prized by expert collectors have changed hands on many oc-

* Paul Jokelson, who writes so poetically of sulphides in his *Sulphides: The Art of Cameo Incrustation,* describes this art of cameo under glass: "drops of rain or dew give a silvery aspect to the leaves which are villous and rough to the touch. From this it has been deduced that an unpolished object which does not melt at the temperature of crystal could, incrusted in its depth, simulate silver."

casions through the years, their values run well into the thousands of dollars. An interesting example is a paperweight we read about which was sold for around $200 at an auction in London in the 1950s. When this same weight was auctioned again three years later, it went for over $1,000, and then again in another few years for over $5,000. Of course, this is most unusual, but we have heard of similar records.

There is a strong revival in collecting weights, but unless you have plenty of money in which to indulge your fancy, it is not likely that you will collect many of the antique Baccarat, St. Louis and Clichy; nor an English Apsley Pellatt (circa 1850) which is difficult to distinguish from a French weight. However, don't despair and give up collecting before you begin, as there are many magnificent paperweights on the market today.

BACCARAT CRYSTAL

Several years ago Baccarat celebrated its bicentennial (1764–1964), and in honor of this occasion produced a very limited edition of a millefiori. Most of these were given to company executives and are no longer available, but, who knows, you may be fortunate enough to come across one in an antique shop or among family possessions (this happens more often than you realize). Today Baccarat is carrying on the art of sulphide paperweight making which they revived about twenty years ago after a lapse of nearly a century. In quoting from a Baccarat brochure:

It all came about at the time of the first Eisenhower presidential campaign. Mr. Paul Jokelson, a French collector who lives in America and became the founder and president of the Paperweight Collectors' Association, prompted Baccarat in Paris to try reviving the making of sulphide paperweights. He presented them with an Eisenhower campaign medal which was then being circulated and suggested that they make a cameo from it. After many tries they finally succeeded . . . one-hundred-and-fifty-three were made.

We have recently seen this paperweight priced at $425 in a dealer's catalogue. At Mr. Jokelson's further urging, the coronation weight was issued in 1953, portraying the Queen and H.R.H. the Duke of Edinburgh (now Prince Philip). The edition was limited to 1492 regular and 195 overlay, and the mold was destroyed in 1959. The cameo was the work of Gilbert Poillerat, a noted French sculptor.

After this sweeping success, Baccarat began seriously again to cater to paperweight collectors with the following releases: Lincoln, 1954; Washington, 1954; Churchill, 1954; Jefferson, 1954; Queen Elizabeth (overlay), 1954; Robert E. Lee, 1954; Benjamin Franklin, 1955; Lafayette, 1955; Martin Luther, 1956; Pope Pius XII, 1960; Sam Rayburn, 1961; John F. Kennedy, 1964; Pope John XXIII, 1965; Theodore Roosevelt, 1967; Will Rogers, 1968; Adlai Stevenson, 1969; James Monroe, 1970; Herbert Hoover, 1971; Eleanor Roosevelt, 1971.

Today's Baccarat prices run around $50 for the regular and $155 for the overlay. Dealers are asking $75 or more for the Adlai Stevenson; $110, Will Rogers; $95, Pope John; $100, Theodore Roosevelt; $225, Lafayette. The quantities of these editions varied with the subjects and the molds have been destroyed. The John F. Kennedy paperweight, 1964, was a great exception with 3,572 regular ($35), 308 overlay ($135) and 314 memorial ($65). All of these are unavailable except on the dealers' market at prices running as high as three to eight times their original cost.

Baccarat originally intended to limit editions of sulphide paperweights to 1,500 regular and 200 overlay. However, the overwhelming popularity of these weights, demonstrated by the constantly increasing number of collectors and advance orders practically selling out every issue before its release, convinced Baccarat to increase the supply somewhat to meet the demand. The issues now are 2,000 regular and 300 overlay. This small increase will never satisfy the demand, and this in itself is one of the things which makes collecting fun.

Baccarat paperweights will always have high market value for several reasons:

(1) Interesting subject matter

(2) Unusual artistic beauty—the work of such prominent French artists as Gilbert Poillerat who is not only a sculptor but a designer of jewelry and a medal engraver; Dora Maar, protégée of Picasso, and the late Albert David, official medalist of the French Mint

(3) Limiting of the editions, certified before a French Notary Public that the molds have been destroyed

(4) Dating of the pieces next to the cameo sculptor's signature inside the crystal so that it cannot be altered or erased

(5) Guarantee of authenticity with a signed certificate by Baccarat inside the satin-lined presentation case which comes with each weight.

Regular sulphides measure approximately 2¾" in diameter and 1½" in height. They are made in clear crystal, cut with five or six facets over a colored background; and not more than two colors are used. The overlays are around 3¼" in diameter and 2 inches in height. Facets are cut generally in an overlay of color over white opaline and the base coated with another color.

There are other Baccarat sulphides made in nonlimited editions including the twelve signs of the zodiac and Our Lady of Lourdes. These and other subjects are produced from time to time in small numbers and sell as quickly as the proverbial "hot cakes." They are priced at considerably less than the limited editions. Millefiori has also returned to the Baccarat scene as they started to make them again around 1958. In purchasing these, be most careful that it is through a reputable dealer and not someone who sells new ones as "antique" Baccarat weights. Two identification marks which have come to our attention are: (1) one cane with the figure "8," and (2) forms of canes bearing the twelve signs of the zodiac in black-and-white opaline.

In the words of M. André Vullict, Executive Vice-President of Baccarat: "Even though the commercial 'millefiori' are not meant to be a limited edition, they are made so beautifully, yet so slowly, at a pace that Baccarat hopes will reach three hundred annually in the next few years, that they will always remain in the collector's field."

Within the reach of everyone interested in paperweights are Baccarat's clear crystal, noted for its brilliance and simplicity of design. In this group are the

Anchor, Diamond, Star and Maltese Cross; each placed on the retail market for $34.

Baccarat paperweights are sold exclusively through selected dealers and for the one nearest you write to Baccarat Crystal, 55 East Fifty-seventh Street, New York, New York 10022.

CRISTAL d'ALBRET

In France another company, formed around fifty years ago, the Cristalleries et Verreries de Vianne (Cristal d'Albret), is now making sulphide paperweights (regular and overlay) in limited editions for Paul Jokelson. We mentioned him previously in connection with Baccarat sulphides; the author of *Sulphides: The Art of Cameo Incrustation;* and founder and president of the Paperweight Collectors' Association. Cristal d'Albret pieces are sold through fine dealers from coast to coast. We have seen them at Saks Fifth Avenue in New York which we mention in passing, merely to give you an idea of their quality.

The Cristal d'Albret sulphides are: Albert Schweitzer, General Douglas MacArthur, Mark Twain, John F. and Jacqueline Kennedy (overlay) and Leonardo Da Vinci. Ernest Hemingway and Paul Revere are the most recent releases and retail at $62. Prince Charles and the moon astronauts are forthcoming. Each is the work of Gilbert Poillerat who created cameos for Baccarat, but since 1965 has been exclusively associated with Cristal d'Albret. Editions are limited to 1,000 and approximately 200 flash overlays which sell for $160. Paul Jokelson told us that there was a Columbus weight which was issued for $55 and now sells through dealers for around $90. "I have no doubt," he said, "that these weights like any other product of fine workmanship and limited edition will be the antiques of tomorrow."

For the sincere paperweight collector membership in the Paperweight Collectors' Association is a *must*. The association issues a regular newsletter and publishes the *Annual Bulletin of the Paperweight Collectors' Association* in a limited edition at $11.50. Truly a collector's item itself as the early numbers are out-of-print. It is a beautiful publication with full-color illustrations and the articles are interestingly written by paperweight experts. In the 1970 issue we particularly enjoyed "A Visit to the Cristalleries de Saint Louis, France" by Gerard Ingold. He tells of his tour with Mr. and Mrs. Paul Jokelson to this famous glassmaking company whose origin goes back to the sixteenth century. We have found that every issue offers invaluable information and immeasurable pleasure.

ST. LOUIS

As previously mentioned this renowned glassmaking firm vanished from the paperweight scene, then returned in 1953 and 1954 with a few new releases of fruits, flowers and vegetables which are difficult to find and extremely costly. Production soon discontinued until 1967 when they returned with a sulphide of Lafayette (edition of 250) for which we have seen in a dealer's catalogue the current asking price of $245. St. Louis is in production with three millefiori limited editions; Mushroom overlay in white, red, pistachio and blue; 100 of each color issued at $210: Dahlia in red, pistachio, blue; 100 of each color issued at $140: Flower in red, yellow; 150 of each color issued at $140. There are no plans of their returning to sulphides. According to Lawrence Selman, collector, dealer, writer: "The new St. Louis weights are of extremely good workmanship and should be good investments." His firm, L. H. Selman Antiques in San Francisco, issues a fine catalogue of *Collectors' Paperweights*.

In addition to Baccarat, Cristal d'Albret and St. Louis there are many other beautiful modern paperweights on the market which include:

WHITEFRIARS GLASS LIMITED (England) has produced paperweights since the mid-nineteenth century in addition to their exquisite stemware. They are made in small quantity and average around $45. Each is signed and dated in a cane in the pattern.

PERTHSHIRE (Scotland), established in 1968, is a small firm, but their paperweights are greatly sought after by collectors. Issues are:

Special Limited Editions   1969, 350 issued $135
                             1970, 150 issued   300
                             1970, (dragon fly)   75

(They are signed "p" with the date and issued with a numbered certificate. Once sold out the design is not repeated.)

Limited Editions 250–350 issued. Price around $40. Dated and/or signed. Numbered certificate. Reissues. The 1971 Christmas Holly paperweight was issued in a limited edition of 200 and retailed for $100.

Line of less expensive weights in the $10–$20 range.

MURANO (Italy) is where most of the mass-produced paperweights come from today. For the most part they are nice decorator pieces, but as Lawrence Selman says, "Become familiar with them as many find their way into antique shops and are knowingly or unknowingly sold as old."

Lawrence Selman also suggests that you keep your eyes open for paperweights made by these modern well-known glass artists: Paul Ysart (Caithness Glass Factory in Wick, Scotland) whose works are of great artistic beauty and are priced around $70 to $150. His earlier pieces are very difficult to find and command really high prices. Most of his weights are signed "PY" in a central cane (often difficult to locate). Charles Kaziun (United States) is the most famous American paperweight maker and glass artist. If you can obtain a 1969 issue of the *Annual Bulletin of the Paperweight Collectors' Association* (you may not be successful as most of the past issues are out-of-print and, as we previously mentioned, they are collectors' items in themselves), you will find his recent creations are shown in color. Kaziun pieces are signed with a gold "k" on the reverse side/or a "k" cane in the design of the weight. Prices begin around $125 or $150. Other American artists are: Francis Whittemore, who is featured in the 1970 issue of the *Annual Bulletin of the Paperweight Collectors' Association*, began his career with rose paperweights and quoting from this same issue of the Bulletin: ". . . it was in 1967 that he started experimenting with the techniques of producing flat set-ups. His first weights of this period have an opaque, dull pink ground, sometimes slightly wrinkled, but the flower, fruit or snake is always recognizable and naturalistic, with the 'W' cane prominently displayed." Whittemore weights average $115 and plateau to $400 or more.

Ronald Hansen is an old-timer in the art of glassmaking and has produced practically every type of weight. Prices vary and $50 or less will buy you a good one. The weights are signed with an "H" cane. Paul Stankard is a new name in the art who produces a small number of flower weights which sell for around $100. An "S" cane is used for the signing. All dealers have informed us that his work is well worth considering. Max Erlacher shows unusual promise, too, with the beautiful paperweights he produces in limited editions of one hundred on order from Paul Jokelson of Cristal d'Albret. He was born in Austria, learned his engraving art with J. & L. Lobmeyr in Vienna and in 1957 joined Corning where he has contributed many outstanding achievements. His works include: the Bird and the Nest, the Cat and the Owl and his latest, American Indian (1971). Each is numbered, dated and initialed by Erlacher.

Steuben glass has a beautiful crystal paperweight decorated with interior threads of white glass swirling around a trapped air bubble, approximately $100. Many of the Steuben crystal pieces themselves make perfect paperweights as each is a work of art.

The strictly budget-minded who may not be in the market for limited and expensive paperweights, do not have to deny themselves the pleasure of collecting. There are many truly modestly priced ones on the market. For example, there is a Kennedy coin-cube paperweight with silver coins dated 1964 which sells for less than $10. We mention this because it has double-value importance: (1) Topical—memorial to President Kennedy whose tragic death occurred in 1963; and (2) 1964 was the last year that all-silver coins were minted.

Kosta (Sweden) introduced last year their annual paperweight family. The first issue: Mother, 1970, and Father, 1971. We consider them modern and amusing, and wonder what the rest of the family will look like. They are fun pieces, but made of good crystal and you can't go wrong for the nominal $15.

Val St. Lambert (Belgium) has a signed paperweight at $10. Choice of designs: American eagle, owl, rose, sailing ship, thistle or caduceus.

Abercrombie & Fitch (New York) offers a paperweight of an owl, made exclusively for them and designed by a friend of ours, Mike Moran. It sells in the neighborhood of $15.

The New St. Clair Glass Works has four sulphide paperweights in the "Assassinated President" series in a limited edition of 1,500 each—Lincoln, Garfield, Kennedy, McKinley. A notarized certificate accompanies each weight. $20 each.

Franklin Mint issues a zodiac medal paperweight of solid brass in clear lucite embedment for less than $10. This was designed by Gilroy Roberts, the dean of American medallic sculptors, best known for his Kennedy portrait on the U.S. half dollar which has become the most popular coin in the world.

The Wedgwood Collectors Society features three special-edition paperweights available to members of the society. Liberty Bell—molded in either blue or black jasper ware. Caduceus—in black jasper ware with the border trim and design work in delicate white jasper. Libra—molded in black jasper ware, trim and design in white jasper ware. Each sells for around $35 to members.

Here are several simple rules to follow in collecting paperweights:

(1) Collect those issued in limited editions.

(2) Look for a date or signature (few old ones had them).

(3) Consider the reputation of the maker and artistic talent of the artist.

(4) Read everything you can on the subject in books and magazines.

(5) Join a club or association which will put you in touch with other collectors.

(6) Pay the prices you can afford and try to obtain some knowledge of potential values.

(7) LAST, and very important—depend upon a recognized paperweight dealer who will keep you informed on current prices and all new issues.

Happy collecting!

CHAPTER IV

MUSIC BOXES

The sound of music boxes holds romantic fascination for young and old. From observation it appears that those who concentrate on these charming collectibles derive more enjoyment than any other type of collector.

"That's because these music-making marvels have tremendous sensory appeal," a collector told us. "You can hear delightful melodies of tinkling bells, beating drums and clashing cymbals. And watch little acrobatic dolls, twirling dancers, singing birds and carousels that go round and round. You intuitively know that friends enjoy your music boxes and never seem a bit bored even when you explain the intricacies of the mechanical precision."

Music boxes originated in Switzerland in the eighteenth century. They really came into great popularity when ingenious watchmakers inserted tiny musical mechanisms in timepieces, rings, jewel boxes and snuffboxes to amuse royalty and the nobility. As time progressed, large and elaborate music boxes were made for homes, cafés and other public places. The rare, old music boxes are the German Symphonium, Polyphon, Kalliope, and the American Regina and Olympia. With the invention of the phonograph ("talking machine," as it was called), music boxes almost disappeared entirely from parlors and became all but a relic of the past. In recent years, however, the music box has made a happy return and beautiful ones with precision Swiss movements are being made today in Switzerland, the United States, Italy, Japan and other countries. They come in a variety of shapes and forms: dancing figurines, powder and jewel boxes, picture plaques, grand pianos, bird cages, Christmas bells and balls, decanters and jugs, alarm clocks and exquisite charms and other pieces of jewelry.

Among the finest modern music boxes we have seen are those made by Thorens and Reuge of Switzerland. In clear, bell-like tones, they run the scale from eighteen notes to the entire range of seventy-two notes. Well-known melodies include: "Liebestraum," "Strangers in the Night," "Blue Danube," "Mozart's Drawing Room," "Try to Remember," "Shadow of Your Smile," "The Sound of Music," "Somewhere My Love" (the haunting song from the famous motion picture, *Doctor Zhivago*), and a variety of other modern tunes, classical airs, folk songs, Christmas carols and lullabies.

If you have never been in a shop specializing in music boxes, an enchanting experience awaits you. Our first visit was to Rita Ford, Inc. (New York), who has probably the greatest dealer collection of music boxes in the

world. On view you will see little modern Swiss novelties
for less than $10 and next to them, perhaps, a stately
antique selling close to $8,000 or the big upright Regina
from the old *Dixie Belle* showboat which once plied up
and down the Mississippi River. Among Mrs. Ford's
modern specialties are custom-made music boxes called
the "His" and "Her" songs ($150 and up). Several years
ago, Mrs. Ford told us, a customer asked her to reproduce
Lara's theme song ("Somewhere My Love") in a music
box as it was his wife's favorite. It wasn't too long before
practically every music-box maker caught on to the idea
and an avalanche of "Lara and her song" flooded the
market. Thus, Mrs. Ford unwittingly became responsible
for the popularity of this modern choice. Be sure to add a
music box playing this tune to your collection as it is
one of the favorite songs of the 1960s. Another Rita Ford
original is the music box playing selections from Stephen
Foster. The hand-carved, custom-made carrousels are one-
of-a-kind music boxes and definitely slated to be among
the antiques of tomorrow.

G. Schirmer, Inc. (New York) one of the best-known
music stores in the country, offers a fine variety of modern
music boxes. Looking at their window display of music
boxes one day, we became very much interested in the
Snoopy, Lucy and other well-known "Peanuts" favorites.
These are recommended collectibles along with any other
outstanding, contemporary comic characters. The "Peanuts" music boxes are inexpensive ($10 or $15); and
though mass-produced and most likely purchased as children's toys, we do not think too many will be around
in the future. Many eventually will be broken and end
up in the junk pile. Others may be kept for sentimental

reasons, but not in working order. Mainly because the owners will not know where to send them for repairs. If you cannot find a shop doing this type of restoration work, our suggestion is to contact G. Schirmer, or Rita Ford whose firm recently restored a bell box, Swiss origin, for the Mark Twain Museum in Hartford, Connecticut.

Comparatively few books have been written about music boxes. *The Curious History of Music Boxes* by Roy Mosoriak (first published in 1943) is reputed to be the first on the subject; and *Collecting Musical Boxes and How to Repair Them* by Arthur Ord-Hume is considered the first new book in decades (1967). The sparse list also includes: *Mechanical Musical Instruments* by Alexander Buchner, *From Music Boxes to Street Organs* by R. deWaard, and *Musical Boxes, A History and an Appreciation* by John E. T. Clark (printed in England, 1948, revised and enlarged in 1952). Much valuable information will be found on music boxes in encyclopedias and general books on antiques. Also keep a watchful eye for newspaper and magazine articles and advertisements as the music box is definitely IN today. A reliable dealer will prove most helpful in your study and collecting. Try to locate one in your vicinity who is a specialist, or at least shows keen interest and is knowledgeable. You will then be prepared to make your first purchase, and take our advice and start off with the best you can afford.

Here are a few suggestions, in addition to the ones previously mentioned: Heavenly Angels, made in Italy by Anri (18-note Swiss musical movement). Around $15. Anri Children music boxes (28-note Swiss movement), approximately $30. Genuine Hummel picture plaques.

Ten different motives, less than $15 each. If you are fascinated by the young children from the drawing board of Juan Ferrandiz, the famous Spanish artist (member of the UNESCO executive committee in Barcelona), you must certainly look for the musical chests with hand-carved wood reliefs, exquisite reproductions of his work. In the neighborhood of $50. These can be ordered by mail through Hildegarde Studios (Hartford, Connecticut). We have found this firm has many fine music boxes; why not send for one of their catalogues?

Every music box collector will be interested in the hi-fi recordings of "Music Boxes from Rita Ford's World Famous Collection," released by Columbia Records. These albums are delightful and demonstrate the variety of sounds from rare, old machines including the large and small kalliope with bells and the deep-throated Regina. They are sold exclusively at record and gift shops and destined to become collector's items in their own right. For the true "music box buff" there is the Musical Box Society Internationale (New York) with approximately a thousand or more members including many from abroad. Members meet, exchange information, listen to music boxes and show slides.

We hope that you will enjoy collecting music boxes. To end this chapter on a light note, we heard the amusing anecdote, which we consider a tall tale (and a bit corny), that Queen Victoria had a small music box attached to the bustle of her gown and each time she sat down it played "God Save the King."

CHAPTER V

AUTOGRAPHS AND MANUSCRIPTS

The collecting of autographs and manuscripts is an interesting, absorbing and important activity and may be entered into as lightly or intensely as one desires. Collecting, as a serious occupation, began in ancient days when the first scholarly men learned to write; and others were taught to read, copy and preserve the erudite holographs.

From these early days man has had in his possession authentic knowledge of the great achievements and momentous events of past civilizations and cultures. This field of collecting, therefore, is of the utmost significance, as it is through the assemblage of autographs and manuscripts that each age contributes its own chapter to the chronicles of history. Only in this manner could we possibly have become acquainted with the wars of the early Romans and Greeks, the teachings of Aristotle and other philosophers, the orations of Cicero, and the speeches of Cato The Elder who with his war cry, "Carthage ought to be destroyed," was the father of the modern slogan. Even the tempestuous love affairs of Cleopatra would have escaped us completely!

Libraries, museums and universities throughout the world are still the capital centers for autograph and manuscript collections, but there are thousands and thousands of private collectors. Never before has there been such a great challenge and opportunity in collecting as today. We are living in the exciting age of action and sound; yet modern communication, made effortless and expeditious by the inventions of the telephone, radio, television, tape recorder, poses no threat to the collector. During the past few decades an abundance of important autographic material has become available from every corner of the earth. Rapidly changing conditions of the world—greater population, higher education, less illiteracy, extensive air travel—play a vital role in opening vast new areas for collecting material which in the past would have remained in obscurity; or, at least, unobtainable to the average person.

Neophytes in every phase of collecting are to be admired, but none more envied than those engaged in autographs and manuscripts. The scope is limitless, and as any collector will tell you, when you begin there is no knowing in advance where or how far your interests and enthusiasm will direct you. It is no idle promise to say that fun, excitement and potential monetary gains await you, but there is a bit of "know-how" necessary to prepare you against the competition of the experts. A few rudimentary suggestions will, we hope, prove helpful.

To the outsider who knows little or nothing about the subject, and often too, the beginning collector, autograph has come to mean "signature." Literally, autograph, derived from the Greek: *autos* (self) and *graphein* (to write) includes: manuscript of a book, poem, song, musical score, document, diary, ship's log, and the most prevalent of all—*letters*. In fact, anything that is written in an individual's own handwriting is an autograph.

The majority of us are probably most familiar with the signature collector who besieges important people in public places with fluttering pen and paper and the request, "May I have your autograph, please?" To the dismay of the conscientious, sincere novice, these hastily scrawled signatures usually end up being worth less than the proverbial "a dime a dozen," and consequently add little to a good collection. Glancing through many dealer catalogues, we often see groups of signatures listed between $35 and $50. To be certain, each is the name of a well-known person, but the entire offering comprises nothing more than a potpourri of names. A good beginning for a beginner, but not of much intrinsic worth to a collection. However, if instead of signature, these same individuals had written letters or anything of an interesting or personal nature (about themselves or the world in general), the collector would have something of value. No one collecting signatures exclusively should be discouraged; nor should he harbor false hopes of obtaining an enviable collection or realizing handsome returns from his efforts. If, however, signature collecting is your interest, devote yourself to it diligently and do not go about it in a hit-and-miss fashion. Robert Notlep, dedicated collector for over twenty-five years, explains this fully in his book, *The Autograph Collector: A New Guide* (Crown Publishers, Inc.). As a boy of twelve he asked Joe DiMaggio to sign a baseball for him. He not only obtained the request from his hero, but went home with the signatures of the entire Yankee team on a sheet of official stationery. This launched him on the collecting of autographs and the adventure emerged into a fabulous collection of over 25,000 signed photographs, cards, books and letters. Today he is an expert in the field and his collection comprises presidents, cabinet members, senators, ambassadors, scientists and notables of every description.

Now, stepping farther into the world of the "pro," the subject matter is very important and a determining factor in value. For example, signatures, letters and writings of Napoleon range from a few dollars to well over a thousand. It has been reputed that he was a prolific writer with more than 20,000 letters and documents to his credit. There is a famous letter to his uncle, Cardinal Fesch, in which he defied papal supremacy, valued on today's market around $1,000. His many penned "Np" sell for about $75. In addition to the subject matter, rarity, date and length are important. However, it must be remembered that the popularity of the writer or the subject itself often supersedes the age of the material. Available recently was a rare letter of Elizabeth I to the king of France, comprising less than one hundred and fifty words in her own writing—valued at $1,000. Then, there was the original manuscript of Elizabeth II's *Log Book of the Kingfisher Patrol, 1st Buckingham Palace Company,* (of the Girl Guides, English equivalent of the American Girl Scouts) compiled in 1939 when the present queen of

England was a young princess—also $1,000. The identical prices of these two items would, in our opinion, be based on: letter of Elizabeth I for its age and rarity; and the manuscript of Elizabeth II for the popularity of the writer and current interest in the contents.

Dealer evaluations, as you will discover, are based around supply and demand. Dominating these essentials are: popularity, importance or prestige of the writer of the autograph or manuscript; contents of the material (date, length, subject matter); and the rarity of the piece.

No one knows exactly what forces prompt the desire to collect in any one field. Should your interest in autographs, however, begin with letters or manuscripts in your possession from well-known personalities, deal with a dealer; get to know him and become his friend. He will gladly appraise your material and discuss with you the advisability of adding to your collection, or dismissing it entirely. Together you will share the excitement of collecting which never subsides either on the part of collector or dealer.

There are many reliable and reputable dealers throughout the country. (See list at the end of book.) The oldest established firm of which we are acquainted is Walter R. Benjamin Autographs, Inc. (1887) in New York. This company is headed by Mary A. Benjamin, daughter of the late Walter R. Benjamin, internationally famous dealer. Miss Benjamin, the first woman to enter this field, is the author of *Autographs: A Key to Collecting*. It is one of the finest books on the subject, written in a scholarly manner; most enjoyable reading and packed with solid information. Walter R. Benjamin Autographs, Inc., has, during its eighty-five years, published *The Collector: A Magazine for Autograph and Historical Collectors,* and issued practically every month. This is a combination magazine-catalogue which is extremely helpful and most interesting, editorially and graphically. Miss Benjamin was most helpful when we discussed prices with her. Hemingway, we found, now sells for $400–$750; a good Dylan Thomas letter around $150; an Agatha Christie for $35; a typewritten Ezra Pound for approximately $120. Nazi leaders are in great demand and a good Rudolph Hess letter is over $100. We saw a fine Stravinsky letter for $150; and an interesting Winston Churchill letter dated 1918 to the Right Honorable Herbert Samuel, M.P., on the subject of "the scheme for the recovery of potash from blast furnace dust" which sounds like an early "recycling" program to us. Also priced at $150.

Another autograph dealer in New York, for whom we have high regard, is Charles Hamilton of Charles Hamilton Galleries, Inc. Mr. Hamilton has written two excellent books: *Collecting Autographs and Manuscripts* and *Scribblers and Scoundrels.* In *Collecting Autographs and Manuscripts,* he covers every phase including: how to build a collection, the way to spot forgeries, signatures by proxy, evaluation, selling, preserving autographs, and the future of autograph collecting. Regarding the future he writes, "As our world expands, more and more we must seek a permanent record for our thoughts and activities— whether in literature, diplomacy, science or business. No technological improvements can replace the written word —the most exact and concise record of man's achievements and the means by which he passes on what he has learned to each succeeding generation. When Bell invented the telephone, some predicted that it would mark

the end of the mails. When Edison devised the phonograph, some said that the spoken word would supplant the
written word. But more letters are written today than ever
before in history."

Charles Hamilton's *Scribblers and Scoundrels* is filled
with action, lively information and thrilling excitement on
every page. It is a vivid account of the author's own personal experiences as a manuscript dealer and auctioneer.
He takes his readers on adventuresome journeys, parrying
blows with the secret service and FBI; tells frankly how
he was deceived into buying stolen letters; and reveals
the fierce censure he received when he placed private
letters of a famous lady on the auction block. There are
chapters on the art of buying from dealers, how to bid
at auctions, and what to collect for investment or profit.
On investment tips, his advice in capsule form is: Diver-
sify and buy the finest; never compromise with quality;
do not put your money in mere signatures or insignificant
scraps; avoid such pitfalls as modern authors and political
figures.

Our dealer friend in Fort Washington, Pennsylvania,
is Bruce Gimelson of Bernard and Bruce Gimelson, Inc.
We hope that he will write a book one of these days as
he is well versed in the field. His enthusiasm for the future
of autograph collecting is encouraging and he gave us
some leads to pass along to you. He mentioned that
Picasso is commanding astronomical prices today and
should continue to do so. Arthur Miller, he feels, is a
potential as his letters, when available, sell for under
$50 and should be worth much more in years to come.
Letters of Hemingway and Steinbeck have already started
to increase in value and a good bet is that they will go

even higher. Movie and stage stars may be of some value in the future, possibly John and Lionel Barrymore and Clark Gable. In the world of music he cites Stravinsky, Leonard Bernstein, Stokowski and Toscanini.

Many dealers issue catalogues and price lists, so always be sure to obtain copies whenever available. These are interesting reading, but you should know something about the terminology or you will be puzzled by the abbreviations which are used to describe the autographic pieces:

ALS   Autograph Letter Signed.
LS   Letter Signed.
DS   Document Signed.
MsS   Manuscript Signed.
NY   No year.
ND   No date.

Hobbies—The Magazine for Collectors runs a regular monthly feature "Autographs," conducted by King V. Hostick. There is a collector's club: The Universal Autograph Collectors Club. The latest address we have is: 3109 Brighton Seventh Street, Brooklyn, New York 11235.

Each collector must decide for himself the kind of material he wishes to collect. The choice is his, but we do hold with those who favor specializing in one or two specific fields. There are many categories: statesmen, stage and screen stars, musicians, authors, artists, members of the United Nations, astronauts, military figures. Specialization, we have been told, more often results in a finer, more valuable collection.

Autograph collecting is personal, human and real. We can think of no warmer manner to describe the subject than that "autographs are people." By preserving for the future the important memorabilia assembled today, it places you and every other collector in the rank of a "twentieth-century" historian. Meantime, you will receive great enjoyment and cultural pleasure. And, a profitable investment, we hope.

CHAPTER VI

BOTTLES

Around the turn of the century Carrie Nation and her zealous henchwomen of the W.C.T.U. (Woman's Christian Temperance Union) literally tossed a fortune away when they went around storming saloons and smashing bottles with their swinging hatchets. Had they known that a bottle-collecting boom was on the way, they would have thrown the "nasty stuff" (their terminology, not ours) down the drain, hoarded the empties and their heirs would be millionaires today. This is not at all far-fetched as the early and rare bottles were hand-blown until the bottle-blowing machine was introduced by Michael J. Owens in 1899. Antique bottles command high prices, often running into hundreds of dollars such as the E. G. Booz cabin, amber, $300. Surprising as it may seem, many of the new collector's bottles are far surpassing the prices of the old.

Ten or fifteen years ago no one ever suspected that the collecting of bottles would develop beyond a pleasurable hobby for men and the mild interest of a few women who wished to arrange their flowers in unique glass containers of golden amber, aqua, brown, green, blue and other colors. These discerning women chose their bottles with care, and washed away the labels (if any) and discarded the ones flagrantly embossed with raised letters, bearing the name of the contents and manufacturer. These were not considered aesthetic enough for the home. The bottles preferred were along the lines of an upsidedown horseshoe with a cloverleaf and the words, "Good Luck," or a Remy Martin Cognac bottle (now around $25) with elegant etched lettering, "Made in France by Baccarat."

It is difficult to estimate the actual number of collectors who are intoxicated (figuratively speaking) by the excitement of bottle collecting of every description. They are legion and run well into the thousands and thousands (Avon collectors alone number over 100,000), and it would require a national house-to-house survey to ascertain the count.

The gamut of collecting runs from the old to the new.

OLD BOTTLES—wine, beer, whiskey, soft drinks, patent medicines, foods, condiments, perfumes, Mason jars and glass milk bottles which came in when milk was no longer sold from huge gallon cans in local stores, and practically went out with the introduction of the carton.

Antique bottle collectors are in a league of their own, and mainly interested in memorabilia with "vintage years" of the empties from around 1850 to the early 1900s. You will find these avid collectors everywhere; digging in the country, searching attics, cellars and junk heaps and browsing around shops, antique shows, flea markets, tag sales and at auctions. We have even spotted them on the New York subways reading a book on the subject, devouring one of the popular collector's magazines, or the *Antique Trader Weekly* which has in each issue page after page on bottles; where to buy, sell or trade. They are a learned group, speak authoritatively about bottles of which many of us have never heard. To the uninitiated, prices may seem incomprehensible. Only an expert collector or dealer can satisfactorily explain what makes a Gibb's Bone Liniment, six-sided, olive green, worth $200; Lighthouse figural, C. T. Morris, amber, quart, $500; and Roher's Wild Cherry Tonic Expectoral, roped corners, light amber, $120. As with every other collectible, supply and demand are of prime significance and determined by the rarity of the item, quality of workmanship, unusuality of design, and importance of the manufacturer.

NEW FIGURAL AND COMMEMORATIVE BOTTLES —these are today's great collector's items which were introduced in the mid-1950s by the James B. Beam Distilling Company to promote liquor sales. This was successfully achieved even to purchases by teetotalers whom we have been told are great admirers and collectors of bottles. Other distillers soon followed suit, and what was called a "fad idea" brought about great new interest in collecting bottles.

JIM BEAM

In 1955 Jim Beam was the originator of the modern figural bottles. The outstanding success is due to Martin Lewin, Beam's Executive Vice-President, and to designer Dave Nissen. E. A. Babka, publisher of the *Antique Trader Weekly*, refers to these two men as the "Fathers of the Figural Bottle Collecting Hobby." Mr. Lewin, a merchandising expert, envisioned the uniqueness of these bottles and knew that they would sell and how to do it. Mr. Nissen designed each of the more than 130 original Beam bottles, including thirty or more in Regal china (1955–early 1971 figures). Mr. Babka in his enthusiasm over these bottles has stated: "Beam has used only Nissen; in fact, should they ever dare to use someone other than Nissen, they might well be faced with a Beam collectors' revolt."

Beam's the First National Bank of Chicago (1964) has long been the most sought after bottle and scored a record when its price reached $2,100. Then along came the Agnew Republican bottle in November 1970 at a $150-plate testimonial dinner for the Vice-President by the Republican National Committee. This bottle, in the shape of an elephant, was made in a limited edition of 200, and the molds were destroyed. One bottle was placed on each table with number 1 going to President Nixon and number 2 to the Vice-President. The remaining 198 were distributed at random. Each bottle, bearing serial number, was accompanied with a certificate of authentication personally signed by Martin Lewin. Names of the original owners are on file in the Beam executive offices for the protection of the recipients as well as future possessors.

In less than three months after this bottle was introduced at the Agnew dinner, we noticed that dealers had it on the market; some asking to buy, others offering to sell for $1,850. We wrote to Mr. Lewin extending our congratulations on the success of this figural, and mentioned our amazement over the price. His answer was: "You are correct that only two hundred Agnew bottles were manufactured. However you are wrong about the price, since the latest quotation that I received for this bottle was over $3,000." This shows the importance of Beam figurals, and how topical, national and world events influence their values. Keep this in mind as other bonanzas are forthcoming.

Jim Beam bottles are manufactured in a variety of shapes, designs, sizes and colors. The categories are well diversified and the series include: executive, political, club, centennial, trophy, state, customer specialties. Prices fluctuate from day to day, and dealer to dealer. However, you won't find too great a marginal difference from the ones quoted in the back of this book. Newspapers and magazines, especially those devoted to collecting, will also keep you up-to-date on prices.

Here is a quick listing to stimulate your interest:

EXECUTIVES

1960	$ 82.95
1956	149.60

STATES

New Jersey	$85.50
Montana	92.50
Maine	10.70
Ohio	16.20
North Dakota	83.00

CENTENNIALS

Alaska Purchase	$ 23.35
Santa Fe	199.10

CUSTOMER SPECIALTIES

Harold's Club, 1969	$125.00
Katz Cat	12.00
Harrah's Club, 1963	539.00

A good book on Beam is: *Beam Bottles* by Al Cembura and Constance Avery; Mr. Cembura is an enthusiastic bottle collector and founded the Jim Beam Bottle Clubs of which there is a national club and at least forty affiliates. Membership is around 20,000–30,000. A dealer will be glad to advise you of the club nearest you. In collectors' catalogues, identification and pricing guides, you will find interesting and valuable information on Beams.

EZRA BROOKS

A good introduction to these fabulous collectibles which have been on the market only since 1968 is *Western Collector's Handbook and Price Guide to EZRA BROOKS Ceramic Decanters* (Western World Publishers, producers of *Western Collector* magazine). The first of the Ezra Brooks Heritage China ceramic figural decanters was the

Flintlock Dueling Pistol (now $6.00–$9.00) and the first specialty decanter, Zimmerman Hat Bottle, was made for the Chicago headquartered store ($14–$20). The Golden Rooster was put up for sale in December, 1969, and sold (full) exclusively at the Nugget Casino in Sparks, Nevada, for $15. A total of six thousand decanters were made and almost instantly unavailable. The Nugget has no more and no more will be made by the Ezra Brooks Company. The resale value has risen dramatically and the decanter is listed among dealers in the range of $140–$200. It was produced in such small quantities and within such limited geographical distribution that it has become one of the greatest collector's items. The enthusiasm for Ezra Brooks has spread across the country and values are constantly increasing. However, prices are still within range of a good round-up for the beginning collector. For under $15 you can obtain any one of these fine collector's pieces: the Potbellied Stove, the Iron Horse, Man O'War, the Arkansas Razorback, California Quail. These should spur you on to add the Katz Siamese Cats ($23–$27), Golden Horseshoe ($64.10), Mr. Foremost ($14.70). Not all bottles are nationally distributed as some are of purely local interest such as the Maine Lobster and the New Hampshire Statehouse.

Ezra Brooks are limited editions. The company's distributional pattern of filled bottles covers seven areas in the United States. No area receives more than 27 per cent of the national distribution. For example, if ten thousand decanters were distributed, the average to each of the areas would be one seventh, approximately 1,428.

One of the great joys of collecting is sharing experiences with other collectors. The National Ezra Brooks Bottle

Club is located in Kewanee, Illinois, and other clubs are located in California, Nebraska, Kansas, Colorado. Each club publishes its own Newsletter.

Ezra Brooks has many unique and unusual designs in the development stage. In the words of H. Silverman, president, Ezra Brooks Distilling Company: "Ezra Brooks will never under any circumstances reissue a bottle the marketing of which has been completed."

LIONSTONE

"Great Guns!" you'll say when you get on the trail of collecting Lionstone figural bottles from the continuing series entitled "Masterpieces of the Old West." Here is the golden west in the spirit of Russell and Remington in fine sculptured porcelain. Lionstone figurines are produced only in limited editions and each production numbers less than five thousand. The molds are destroyed and Lionstone guarantees that these pieces will never be reissued. It's a rugged series with excellent portrayals of Sheriff, Gentleman Gambler, Gold Panner, Jesse James, the Sodbuster, Stagecoach Driver, Bartender and other frontier characters. The majority of these are in the hands of collectors and dealers. (See Valuations in Appendix.)

"Lionstone Birds" are a bold departure from the Masterpiece figurines and the first of this new series was the Roadrunner released in the state of Colorado. Fifteen hundred pieces were manufactured and the empties now in dealer's hands run around $40. The Arizona Gambel Quail was the second in the series, introduced in Arizona and priced at $32.95 before release. Other state birds will continue the series.

It has been estimated that there are over a hundred

"bottle clubs" in the United States and among the newest is Lionstone Bottle Collectors of America, Los Angeles, California.

FRANKFORT

A new and interesting series of figural bottles, "American Patriots," has been introduced by Frankfort Distillers Company. They are in limited editions and the molds are destroyed after the first castings. This commemorative series begins with the hand-cast ceramic figures of George Washington and Benjamin Franklin. The retail price (filled) is around $13. They have become much-desired collector's items.

For those interested in astrology, Frankfort has produced in limited quantity a unique edition of sculptured zodiac figures. This series comprises six ceramic figures in all, each bearing complementary signs of the zodiac on the front and reverse sides. The colors range from the golden bronze of Aquarius-Leo to the pale blue of Gemini-Sagittarius. Approximately $15 (filled) was the introductory price.

The first edition of Frankfort's new "Sportsmen" series was in honor of Father's Day, 1971. It's an amusing multi-colored decanter of a golfer, forced to make his approach from behind a tree, approximately $15 (filled) and produced in limited quantity. A good addition to a collection.

GRENADIER

Everybody loves a parade of "Grenadier Soldiers!" They're brave and proudly on review as Grenadier (subsidiary of E. Martinoni) entered the collecting field with an entirely different approach from Beam, Brooks and others. Although proud of the contents, they admit they are selling the decanters.

The parade of these figurals began in 1969 and the editions are limited to less than five thousand, and then the master molds are destroyed. Napoleon and his staff (Lassal, Ney, Eugène, Lannes, Murat) were the first Grenadier soldiers, and quickly sold out after issue (around $15–$20 when available). In this initial series there were six other figurines among which the 1st Pennsylvania Regiment 1775 of the American Revolutionary Army Regiment (about $20 when available) is most difficult to collect as the state of Pennsylvania purchased one third of the total pieces.

The second series (1970–71) includes First Officer's Guard 1804–Napoleonic Regiment and Dragoon 17th Regiment 1812–Napoleonic Regiment and were released (filled) at $17.95.

Each hand-painted porcelain figure is accurate in every detail of uniform, arms and color. A miniature series is planned to meet what Michael Spina, National Sales Manager of E. Martinoni Company wrote us: "Exact replica of an already existing larger bottle not more than two ounces in content or roughly six inches in height."

Collectors of Grenadier soldiers, in the spirit of comradeship, have begun to form their own clubs: There is the Mile High Grenadier Club; and the National Grenadier Porcelain Bottle Club of America.

DOUBLE SPRINGS

In 1970 the "Rare Old Collectors" series of antique cars was presented by Double Springs Distillers, Inc. The initial piece was the 1913 Cadillac Y-6, followed by the Stutz Bearcat, 1919 (both $19.95), and the 1910 Model-T Ford ($24.95). This series is a long-range program to memorialize in handcrafted porcelain some of the world's most famous motor cars. Series will include vintage models such as Dusenberg, Cord and Auburn; and foreign classics including Rolls-Royce, Bentley and Mercedes. Each is a limited edition and the molds are destroyed. It was interesting to learn that the release of the Model-T Ford was made at the Annual Banquet of the Model-T Ford Club International. It will be even more interesting to follow the success of this particular bottle as the "old Tin Lizzie" will always be held in high esteem by collectors of Americana.

If you are unable to find the "Rare Old Collectors" series in your area, write to Double Springs Distillers, Inc., P. O. Box 6087, Louisville, Kentucky 40206. This invitation appeared in an advertisement in the *Antique Trader* (December 29, 1970).

BLACK AND WHITE

The "Black and White Scotties" which Black & White Scotch introduced in their first specialty bottling in authentic bone china (Royal Adderley, Stoke-on-Trent, England) have become blue ribbon winners in many a collection. Price was $40 (filled), but once the contents are emptied they do show up now and then on the dealer's market.

BALLANTINE

The Ballantine's Scotch Collector originals, made of genuine Palfrey china, are of special interest as they celebrate significant aspects of Scottish history and traditions. Since the product is made in very limited supply, it is not possible to issue more than a limited edition of each piece. The molds are destroyed after each run is completed.

The series consists of the Scottish Knight; the Golf Bag*; the Mallard Duck; the Seated Fisherman, and the Zebra. Each figural is authentic in detail and a faithful portrayal of the original subject. In the present dealer's market, each is priced around $15.

J. W. DANT

History comes to life with the introduction of the "Americana" series of fine bottles by J. W. Dant which commemorate celebrated episodes. The first six pieces of the collection are: the Boston Tea Party (milk-white opal glass); the Alamo (African-ebony glass); Constitution & Guerriere (pewter-gray marbleized glass); Patrick Henry (buff marbleized glass); the American Legion 50th Anniversary (cobalt-blue glass). These are issued in limited number and when the supply is exhausted, there will be no more. Dealers list them between $5.00 and $15.

A new series of special bottlings for collectors is "Field Birds"—eight feathered subjects in milk-white opal glass with vivid colors fired in: Ring-necked Pheasant, Chukar Partridge, Prairie Chicken, Mountain Quail, Ruffed

---

* (Merely, as an aside.) In doing our research for this book, we have devoured many tidbits of information. "Caddie" on the golf course derived its name from the days when Mary, Queen of Scots, played at St. Andrews and her royal cadets carried her clubs around the green.

Grouse, California Quail, Bobwhite and Woodcock. These have appeal not only for bottle collectors, but those interested in art. The illustrations were executed by noted nature artist Arthur Singer, hailed as a true successor to John James Audubon. Each bottle will be dated and inscribed with a special collector's indicia. Limited editions are around $10 when available. Other Dant bottles are Boeing 747, Speedway 500, Fort Sill and Mount Rushmore (latter two are ceramics). We consider these a most promising collection.

FAMOUS FIRSTS

Not long on the market, but in a relatively short period the firm of Famous Firsts has aroused the interest of collectors and dealers. They are not produced by a manufacturer of wines and spirits, but solely for the collecting field. Each bottle ($15–$25) is ceramic-cast and the subjects are widely diversified: Marmon Wasp, DeWitt Clinton, Spirit of St. Louis, Renault Racer, French Telephone, Lombardy Scales, Victorian Phonograph, Sewing Machine, Yacht America (up to $75) and figurals of Napoleon, Garibaldi, Bersaglieri, Centurion, Don Sympatico. We particularly appreciate the imagination and love of antiquity which led to the creation of the Bell of St. Paul (the miraculous bell which was cast into the sea by Roman soldiers, swallowed by a fish and rescued when the fish was caught); and the Lombardy Scales (faithful replica of the one used in the countinghouse of the Duke of Medici to weigh out the annual levies and tributes paid by fiefs and subjects).

OLD AND NEW AVONS

Avon's story goes back to 1886 when a door-to-door book salesman, D. H. McConnell, changed his line to perfume and established the California Perfume Company, Inc. Other products including face powder, soap, creams, talcum and lotion were added, and women representatives brought these items to homes in every state of the union. The company really began to grow when cosmetics were accepted. In 1929 the name was changed to Allied Products and then to Avon Products in 1939.

Bottles of the California Perfume Company are greatly sought after by collectors. The Trailing Arbutus Set runs around $300–$350; Daphne Sachet, $75–$85; Lotus Cream, $175–$225; Men's Traveling Kit, $100–$125.

There are Avon bottles in practically every shape, size and form; in glass, ceramics and plastics. The figurals include automobiles, clocks, helmets, dolls, comic characters, birds, fish and animals.

Stuart's Book on Avon Collectables (Lynn R. Stuart, Gilbert, Arizona 85234) is the easiest and quickest way we know for the beginner collector to become acquainted with Avons. It illustrates over five hundred items in black and white, and many in color. Published in 1971, each is priced according to the current market, ranging from $2.00 for '70 Gentlemen's Selection to others from $100 up. Glancing through the book and pretending that we had $50 for an initial collection, we would come up with an interesting variety: '62, Rose Bud, $6.00; '67, Greek Warrior (helmet), $12; '65, First Down (football),

24. Holiday Plates Series, courtesy *the Antique Trader Weekly*.

25. Christmas 1971 Angel Plate by Spode.

26. Haviland Prolongeau Figurines.

27. Artist Girl by Laszlo Ispanky, courtesy Armstrong's.

28. Birds by Royal Copenhagen.

29. Bunny by Royal Copenhagen, courtesy Georg Jensen, Inc.

30. Figurines by
Royal Copenhagen,
courtesy Georg Jensen, Inc.

31. "Saturday," Royal Worcester
Days of the Week Figurines.

32. "Sunday," Royal Worcester
Days of the Week Figurines.

33. Duke of Wellington Figurine
by Bernard Winskill for
Royal Worcester.

34. Doris Lindner's
Holstein Fresian Bull
for Royal Worcester.

35. Blue Marlin by
Ronald Van Ruyckevelt
for Royal Worcester.

36. Royal Worcester's Mayflower Commemorative Ashtray.

37. Plymouth Bowl by Royal Worcester.

38. Mayflower *Compotier* by Wedgwood.

40. Hammersley Annual Bell, 1971, courtesy Spode, Inc.

39. Beethoven Portrait Medallion in Black Basalt by Wedgwood.

41. Christmas "Prancing Horses" by Haviland, photo by Robert Villeneuve.

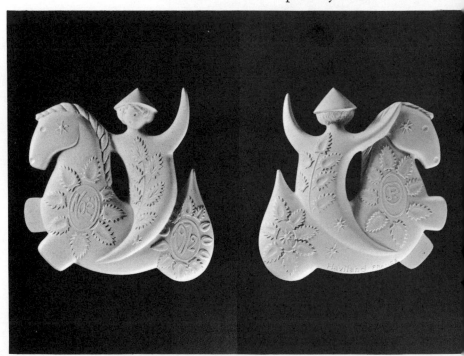

42. Royal Doulton 1971
Christmas Mug,
courtesy Latama, Inc.

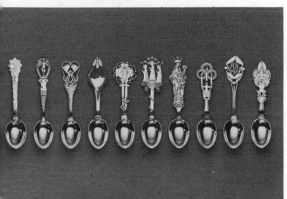

43. Danish Christmas
Spoons by A. Michelsen,
Copenhagen.

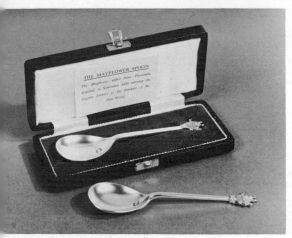

44. Mayflower
Commemorative Spoon
by Royal Worcester.

45. Tiffany Dessert Spoons in the Chrysanthemum, Feather Edge and Audubon Patterns.

46. 1970 Royal Worcester Silver Spoon and Fork.

47. Christmas Spoon and Matching Fork, 1970, by A. Michelsen, Copenhagen.

$5.00; '70, Spirit of St. Louis, $10; '69, Snoopy Decanter, $5.00; '65, Stein, $10; '69, Cologne (½ oz.), $2.00. Exactly $50 and seven fine pieces!

Lynn Stuart also wrote *Collector's Guide to Avon Figural Bottles*. Illustrations are in color. This was a tremendous success, and when it became impossible for him to answer every letter personally which arrived each day in a flood of mail, the idea of the International Avon Collectors Club was formed. Headquarters are at Mesa, Arizona 85201. The club publishes a monthly Newsletter and has issued its first Annual (1969–70).

Avon clubs are sprouting everywhere. And, Bud Hastin's National Avon Club is in Kansas City, Missouri. Mr. Hastin is the author of *Avon Bottle Encyclopedia* which is highly recommended reading.

When you hear "Avon calling" at your door or on TV, that's a reminder of a good line of products and your opportunity to purchase an interesting bottle for a collection or resale.

COCA-COLA

Collectors of Cola-Cola memorabilia and bottles have always had a real thing going for them. Since these collectors are a serious, quiet group who do not widely broadcast their activities, it is difficult to determine how many there are. We found no clubs or associations and very little printed material on the subject.

The Coca-Cola Company has been most helpful, however, in supplying us with interesting, informative data. An excellent treatise is *A Catalogue of Metal Service Trays and Art Plates Since 1898* by Wilbur G. Kurtz, Jr., who heads Coca-Cola USA's Archives Department in Atlanta, Georgia. Several good articles on Coca-Cola appeared in the *Western Collector,* a terrific magazine which should be on every collector's subscription list. In the 1971 January/February Issue, there was an excellent article entitled "Coca-Cola" by Cecil Munsey, author of *The Illustrated Guide to Collecting Bottles* (Hawthorn Books). Mr. Munsey is also writing a book dealing with all aspects of collectibles for Coca-Cola.

Although bottles for Coca-Cola are highly prized, they are a mere part of the collecting story. Artifacts have become so important that Coca-Cola bottlers have established small museums which have instigated new, lively interest in the collecting world.

One has only to glance through the "Merchandise For Sale" column in the *Antique Trader Weekly* to discover the broad category of collectibles. It is an endless parade of Americana which includes serving trays, bottle openers, pencils, miniature bottles, glasses, books, key chains, cuff links, playing cards, calendars, toys, dolls and advertising signs. Prices range from less than a dollar to over a thousand dollars for display items.

Coca-Cola has traveled a long way since 1886 when the first glass was sold at the soda fountain of Jacobs' Drug Store in Atlanta. It is estimated that over 140 million Cokes are consumed around the world each day.

OTHER BOTTLE COLLECTIBLES

Bottle collecting is exciting, challenging and endless. We have merely touched the surface to whet your appetite (for empties, of course) and get you started on your collecting.

In your search don't miss:

BARSOTTINI	Monk with a Wine Jug	$12.10
	William Tell	14.95
	Lamplighter	22.50
	Tivoli Clock	20.95
McCORMICK	Jupiter 60 Mail Car,	
	Passenger Car, Wood	
	Tender, Locomotive.	
	Each less than	15.00
BISHOFF	Red Clown	40.00
	Jungle Scene	33.00
	Senorita	35.00
GARNIER	Clown	60.00
	Napoleon on	
	Horse	21.50

Just for the fun of it and as a mascot to stand guard over your collection there is Mr. Bottle Collector and his wife, Mrs. Bottle Collector, a series issued by the *Antique Trader Weekly* in a limited edition, less than $20 each.

We hope that you've enjoyed this "Here's How" of bottle collecting!

CHAPTER VII

BANKS—STILL AND MECHANICAL

"A penny saved is a penny got." (*Henry Fielding*)
"Penny for your thoughts." (*Jonathan Swift*)
"Penny-wise and pound-foolish." (*Robert Burton*)

As you can see a penny once had its days of great importance. And, too, "Penny Banks" which were originally invented as children's toys were found in almost every home. Today they are leading collectibles.

Still banks (without motion) came first, prior to the manufacture of the mechanicals around 1880 (movable and often with sound). Stills were inspired by the home-made varieties of cutting a narrow slot in the top of a box or glass jar. Many were lettered with the name of a child, hand-painted and even colorfully decorated if a member of the family had artistic talent.

When still banks appeared on the market, they met with instant success and were sold in toy shops and the once-upon-a-time "5¢ & 10¢" stores (Woolworth was one). The castings, in tin or cast iron, were excellent and the fine sculptured detail included nursery-rhyme and comic-strip characters, clowns, Santa Claus, cats, dogs, elephants, lions and pigs. The pig appeared to be the most popular, and you found him sitting, standing and named, Bismarck Pig, Decker's Iowana Pig and Thrifty Pig. Then along came the Piggy Bank with which we are all familiar. Many stills were also made of pottery, glass and papier-mâché.

Banks rank among the first of the educational toys. They taught children how to count and instilled lessons of thrift. Most instructive were the safes, cash registers and ten-cents adding-machine banks. Few of the early banks had trap doors to remove the coins, and the safe banks, in particular, brought torments when the number sequence of the dial combination was either forgotten or lost. Consequently many were broken by the eager hands of the children (mamas and papas, too!) who attempted to release the money. This abuse and mutilation account to a large degree for the few old banks in existence today. And, too, production was in relatively small quantity, and scarcity has really made them desirable and valuable collectibles.

The mechanical banks, naturally, offered the greatest fun and entertainment. The exciting action brought an immediate reward for saving pennies. By placing a coin in the hand of Humpty Dumpty (or some other character), you could see him pop it in his mouth, roll his eyes and beg for more; or in mystifying suspense watch a penny disappear from under the hat of a magician. It was usually as simple as that, as the coin inserted in the slot triggered off the action of a lever. Automation later advanced to battery-operated banks.

Topical interest has always influenced the designs for banks. Among the popular mechanical antique banks are: Teddy and the Bear (1907), Punch and Judy (1882), Creedmore and Soldier (1877), Uncle Remus (1890). Harlequin and Columbine, and Freedman's Bank top the mechanical bank list as they have been privately owned and under wraps for years and seldom change hands. Prices for old mechanicals range from around $35 to over $3,000 (the latest price we have seen quoted for Harlequin and Columbine). Stills run from $20 up.

Modern banks fall into the "1935 and on category," according to F. H. Griffith, private collector and for over twenty years editor and feature writer of "Old Mechanical Banks" in *Hobbies*. The variety of the subjects in stills and mechanicals is wide: radio, refrigerator, television, jukebox, two-car garage, Jack Benny's bank vault, Mr. Peanut Vending, Lone Ranger, trolley car, automobiles, airplanes, Yellow Cab, war tanks, battleships, mail boxes, helicopter—name it and you will probably find it in the form of a bank.

We asked Mr. Griffith his expert opinion on what banks being made today will become the antiques of tomorrow. Readily he answered: "Since 1935 there have been many mechanical banks made and there are numbers still being made today, mostly in plastic and some metal. As an example, mechanical banks having to do with space travel are of considerable interest. All of these types will be collectors' items of the future." He speaks as a mechanical bank specialist, but we feel certain that the same advice is applicable to still banks.

Here are a few suggestions to aid you in assembling a collection of present-day banks:

(1) Favorite comic-strip characters whose popularity you feel will survive in the same manner as the old banks fashioned after Buster Brown and Tige; Mickey Mouse; Mutt and Jeff; Donald Duck. Peanuts and his pals: Snoopy, Lucy, Charlie Brown, Schroeder, etc., head the list at this time.

(2) Well-known personalities—the old ones featured George Washington, General Pershing, Teddy Roosevelt, Ben Franklin. Later ones are Charlie Chaplin and Jack Benny. Unfortunately, we haven't come across any others, but if you do, snatch them up.

(3) Any new invention such as the computer (radio, television, telephone, refrigerator are past examples).

(4) Automobiles—always a good bet for the bank collector and car buff.

(5) Space—best group of all. Collect whatever you can find on rockets, flying saucers, moon flights.

Space banks are the leaders. Apollo 8, the first space ship to the Moon, was in limited production, and if you come across one, purchase it by all means. The Apollo U.S.A. is a commemorative cast-iron bank produced as a tribute to all Apollo moon flights and belongs in every collection. Less than $10.

Worthy of consideration is a musical bank of the

Capitol which plays the "Star-Spangled Banner" and has the photographs and names of every president of the United States. This is also a limited edition and retails around $15. It is unique items of this nature which will start you on the road to an interesting collection.

The Snoopy Doghouse bank sells for less than $5 and as a collectors' item it should become a perennial favorite along with Mickey Mouse and Donald Duck which are constantly appearing in new versions. Banks are still primarily manufactured under the classification of Toys, so browse around the toy stores for the newest creations.

Many fine reproductions are presently being made of the old still and mechanical banks. We have discovered that collectors in general do not give too much importance to these replicas. However, our opinion is based on the premise that "What was *new* yesterday is old today, and what is new today will be *old* tomorrow." In most instances, the word "reproduction" is frightening as it infers "mass production." In the case of banks, it is safe to assume that the market will never be flooded, as the saving of pennies (nickels, dimes, even quarters) retains little of the importance of days gone by. And, since comparatively few of the old banks are available, good reproductions should not be entirely ignored.

Before beginning to collect banks, it might be a good idea to learn something about the old stills and mechanicals. This will initiate you into the wide scope of the subject; and acquaint you with the values of the old banks and the potentials of those currently manufactured.

Old Iron Still Banks by Hubert B. Whiting describes

and illustrates in color over four hundred and fifty of the early and important banks. *Mechanical Bank Booklet* by F. H. Griffith is an informative handbook on American and foreign mechanical banks. Both authors are collectors and grade the banks for their rarity and relative value. If they were dealers, they would do it differently, presumably by price lists which fluctuate greatly through supply and demand. *Toy Bank Reproductions and Fakes* by Robert L. McCumber and *Old Penny Banks* by Meyer and Freeman are also suggested reading. You can follow the banking market and news in *Hobbies* and the *Antique Trader*.

Collect for the fun of it, but keep this in the back of your mind. If the North Pole bank has reached around $800, Little Joe and William Tell $275 and a combination safe $25, it certainly seems that today's Moon Landing banks will eventually rocket in value.

CHAPTER VIII

DOLLS AND TOYS

"How dear to this heart are the scenes of my childhood." With pleasant recollections of many things past, we share with Samuel Woodworth (1785–1842) his feelings of nostalgia as expressed in the opening line of "The Old Oaken Bucket." These words seem appropriate as an introduction to dolls and toys.

Dolls and toys date back to prehistoric times. Their ingenious invention to amuse children intuitively sprung from watching the wild young animals romp and play with sticks and stones. Among the archaeological discoveries of Egyptian, Greek and Roman civilizations are children's toys made of bone, wood, clay, iron, bronze and gold. The list includes balls, tops, boats, kites, birds, chariots, horses and other animals; and dolls, even with movable arms and legs which were securely fastened with pegs. Each successive era has made its own important contribution to this essentially pristine manner of entertaining and educating children.

Playthings from ancient days are primarily in museums around the world or in private collections. They are well worth investigating and studying by everyone engaged in this field of collecting. Those in circulation are for the most part from the late Victorian period. Even though the toy industry in this country and abroad was flourishing in the 1800s, items are rare due to the attrition of hard usage and the sad fact that dolls and toys are generally either given away or discarded on the junk heap when children grow up.

Collectors are numerous; their legion is steadily increasing and collecting is a well-established endeavor with both men and women. In this turbulent age there are times when we all feel that "the world is too much with us." Collecting in every field is a sane escape from reality and tension, and dolls and toys are an especially quieting panacea. Entertaining, appealing and fascinating, they are wholesome, psychological flashbacks to the natural, happy pleasures of past childhoods, our own and others.

Among the dolls and toys which are being manufactured today, the scope is broad and the choice is wide. Many are indeed destined to find their deserving place with the treasured relics of the past. As you enter this fascinating field of collecting, we offer a few suggestions:

(1) Begin by obtaining all the background knowledge possible on the history of dolls and toys. In this manner, you will familiarize yourself with the

subject, and quickly recognize that the basic characteristics have not changed throughout the ages.

(2) Keep in mind the age in which we are living. Toys developed around space travel, monorails, new inventions, popular comic characters, and every other timely subject reflect contemporary life and will become the antiques of tomorrow.

(3) Make it a habit to browse around toy departments. Talk to the parents of young children about toys. In this way, you will learn firsthand what is new and different.

(4) Collect with discernment and what you assemble today will very likely have historic interest and considerable value as time goes on!

DOLLS

The collecting of dolls ranks with every other top hobby. Your first note of encouragement is that antique dolls command high prices, and there is every reason to suppose that within a comparatively short time modern dolls will manifest equal or better values. Collectors of antique dolls will tell you that the old French Jumeau runs in the neighborhood of $200–$600; the Schoenhut, made in America after World War I by a German immigrant, is around $50–$150. Gibson Girls have reached as high as $800. In actuality, these are not genuine antiques as the general ruling is a hundred years old. However, because of the scarcity of old dolls, collectors and dealers, even museums, are willing to accept them as articles of historical significance, regardless of age.

Our choice among the many beautiful and interesting

modern dolls begins with Madame Alexander dolls. These are most worthy collectibles and will be passed along from generation to generation in the same tradition as the Jumeau and Eden Bebe dolls. The Alexander Doll Company, founded in 1923, was the brain child of Madame Alexander whose parents established the first doll hospital in the United States before the turn of the century. When initially produced, these dolls were made of cloth with dimensional facial features. They created great attention as being a clever departure from the old-fashioned rag dolls with flat faces.

The early Alexander creations, "Dolls from the Classics," began a trend which has continued in the company's selection of doll characters. Madame Alexander is a firm believer that a doll is more than a cuddly plaything and that it should be true to life and introduce a child to favorite fictional characters and actual people. Excellent examples are Little Women (Marmee and her four daughters, and Laurie, the handsome boy who married Amy); Scarlett O'Hara (*Gone With the Wind*); and the two Jenny Lind dolls, inspired by Frances Cavanah's books.

The "Dolls from Storyland" is a series which includes Mary Mary, Red Riding Hood, Hansel, Gretel, Bo-peep, Miss Muffet. The "Portrait Dolls" are such faithful and masterly creations that one almost feels they have stepped out of a Godey print or Renoir canvas.

There are baby dolls of every description and Sweet Tears is terrific. She drinks, wets and weeps. Mary Cassatt Baby is the newest and we are certain would be a joy to the great nineteenth-century artist whose work inspired this creation.

"The International Dolls" are from many lands and dressed in their native costumes. They are already collectors' delights and at the United Nations Day celebration, October 22, 1965, the complete line was on display. Madame Alexander dolls are truly museum pieces. They have been on exhibit at the Brooklyn Children's Museum (New York), Museum of the City of New York and the Children's Trust Museum in New Delhi, India; in addition to many local museums throughout the United States. There is a permanent exhibit at the Congressional Club, Washington, D.C.; and a presentation was made to the Smithsonian Institution, Washington, D.C., of Madame Doll, portraying the Revolutionary period, and the famous Scarlett O'Hara of the Civil War era. At the present time, Madame Alexander dolls retail from $10–$50.

The Barbie dolls (Mattel, Inc.) made their debut as teen-agers around fifteen years ago and they deserve every collector's recognition. Barbie, Francie, Stacey and Ken are each less than $10 but it is the wardrobe, sold separately, which makes parents think they are highly expensive. They are a very dressy group and have outfits for every occasion. Collectors must keep this in mind, as each garment or piece of clothing is intrinsically important. Doll's clothes depict a period of time, and dolls wearing miniskirts, bikinis, pants suits will, in the future, join the ranks of the official reporters of what styles were like in the 1970s. The Barbie dolls have an English cousin, Sindy. She's really something with her smart sports car, a fashion catalogue showing her clothes and her own fan club, "The Sindy Club." Her attractive boyfriend is Paul. Every serious Barbie collector should have the British version, and to keep expenses down let them borrow each other's clothes.

The imported Ilaria dolls are exquisite and worthy of becoming collectors' treasures. We have admired one elegantly dressed in velvet with sheer pantaloons, white parasol and long feathered boa. Price approximately $25.

There are dolls and dolls of every description. Several recent ones from England which struck our fancy are the Portrait dolls of a commemorative nature (priced less than $15) by famed dollmaker, Peggy Nisbet:

(1) Prince Charles, attired in his royal robes for investiture as Prince of Wales.

(2) Queen Elizabeth II in her ceremonial costume of "The Most Ancient and Most Noble Order of the Thistle."

(3) Sir Winston Churchill, as pompous and hearty as we recall him.

Mary Poppins (Peggy Nisbet doll) herself has flown in from England! What a quaint sight she must have been on a 747 plane, dressed in her nanny outfit, complete with carpetbag and parasol. Less than $10.

In assembling your collection, it is advisable to keep abreast of current trends as manufacturers are quick to produce dolls of universal appeal. Just recently those old-time favorites, Raggedy Ann and her playmate, Raggedy Andy, have made a terrific comeback. These floppy, button-eyed, rag dolls have been with us for more than fifty years and for a while they seemed to have been forgotten. Then, suddenly ZOOM, they are in every toyshop as adorable and lovable as ever. Now they are smart, little celebrities with their happy, smiling faces on greeting cards, books, clothing, jewelry, bed and bath linens, puzzles and games. In fact, we have read that they endorse over four hundred advertised products. Real "Mod," too, with zippers and buttons, and even one model with a concealed Swiss music box. At the United States Pavilion at Canada's Expo '67 they were given the honor of being referred to with great respect as the "American Folk Doll." In replying to the message "I Love You" in a heart design on every Raggedy Ann, everybody seems to have the same answer, "We love you, too!"

Spacemen, doctors, nurses, television and movie stars, comic characters—these are all of topical interest and belong in every collection. The trolls from Denmark and the leprechauns from Ireland are strange, weird little creatures who are supposed to bring good luck, and are inexpensive enough to add a few, if for no other reason than guardian mascots of your collection.

Ventriloquist dolls are fascinating. But since there aren't many ventriloquists, there aren't many of these character dolls. Charlie McCarthy, Mortimer Snerd, Danny O'Day and Lester, who for many years have won the hearts of young and old, are still the leaders (around $15–$20).

An excellent addition to a doll collection is a handmade, stuffed doll dressed in the costume of a Colonial Williamsburg hostess.

DOLLHOUSES AND FURNISHINGS

Every collector of modern dolls should have a dollhouse, preferably contemporary in style—ranch, two-family, apartment, A-frame, condominium. There are very attractive ones with stone terraces, garages with sliding doors, electric lights, bathrooms and kitchens, wall-to-wall carpeting. Furnishings include: television sets, refrigerators, double sinks, pieces for the dining room, bedroom, living room and patio. They tell today's story, and deserve preserving; many, undoubtedly, becoming valuable heirlooms of tomorrow.

TOYS

If there is truth in the old adage, "Every man is a boy at heart," then no wonder toy collecting has become especially popular with men. The male collector will go about his hobby in a precise, methodical manner and he will knowledgeably specialize in one or two categories such as electric trains, automobiles, space travel.

We've been around the shops and pored endless hours through toy manufacturers' catalogues and the horizon is promising for collecting tomorrow's antiques. Your own judgment and vision will tell you which of the toys are worthy collectibles. We'll start your thinking with trains, stuffed animals, musical sleep toys, puppets and all the delightful items associated with Peanuts, Snoopy and Charlie Brown.

Lionel electric trains have traveled a long way since they were introduced in the early 1900s. In 1970, Model Products Corporation (Mount Clemens, Michigan) obtained the rights to manufacture and sell Lionel trains. Production is on the right track with new sets and vast improvements in motor, wheels and visual appeal. A unique and exciting innovation is the authentic sound of a chugging steam engine with white puffing smoke from the locomotive. Silver Star and the Overlander are the two sets with this feature and retail reasonably. Many of the trains come with villages to place around the tracks, engineers, firemen and brakemen. The accessories are fantastic—billboards (Cheerios, Betty Crocker, Sheraton Hotels & Motor Inns, etc.), automatic crossing gates and signals, trestles, bridges, freight-station platforms, watchman's shanties, switch towers, water tanks and other realistic structures. We feel there's definite potentiality in the freight cars which bear the big names in American industry—Hershey Chocolate, Sunoco, Wheaties. The piggyback and refrigerator cars mark twentieth-century progress in railroading.

For train information on the Lionel line, we traveled many happy journeys. One of the first stops was reading a colorful brochure issued by Lionel trains and priced around $1. Our most exciting experience was a visit to Model Railroad Equipment Corporation (New York) who specialize in Lionel trains. Here, we viewed antique trains and watched the new ones running. What we specifically learned is that the antique Lionels sell from $4.00 to $1,000. Then, we glanced at the *Illustrated Lionel Checklist 1929–70* (Ladd Publications, Inc., Evanston, Illinois 60204). Here are the few prices we jotted down (hurriedly, so we would not miss our own train back to Connecticut):

> *Pennsylvania*
> 1948 $37.50 list price
> 1950   37.50 "   "
> 1955   49.95 "   "
> *Great Northern*
> 1960   75.00

Union Pacific

1950	35.00
1955	18.50
1969	18.50

The book is illustrated and at random we picked a few years—mainly to inform you of this manual. List prices, naturally, are determined by (1) the material used in manufacture, (2) the model itself (coach, engine, baggage car, etc.), (3) buying power of the dollar.

If you are interested in a club, there is the Train Collectors Association in Pittsburgh, Pennsylvania.

For the collector who is willing to assemble his own Honda or Thunder Chopper, trucks, autos, race cars and space ships (or has a son who will do it for him), Model Products has a fabulous variety of scale kits. These superdetailed models offer a fast and inexpensive way to build up an interesting collection. They're sure to have great historical importance.

Here's a list of other modern toys which deserve due consideration:

School Buses
Gas and Service Stations
Garage and Heliport
Aircraft Carriers
Ski Lifts
Yacht Clubs
Ranches
Supermarkets
Playgrounds

In the miniature world are Corgi Toys, Dinky Toys and Matchbox (imported from England). You'll be bewildered by all the collectibles available, but don't worry about mass production. Toys will always be short-lived, and most of the ones kids are playing with today will be gone tomorrow. If you select wisely it won't be long before your collection will have value.

Of course, everything to do with Peanuts and his friends—games, mobiles, dolls, watches and clocks, books. Start off with the soft white plush and huggable Snoopy, the puppy with the floppy black ears ($12 for 19" and $35 for 30"). These characters are going places—and will surpass Sparkplug, Barney Google, Mickey Mouse, Donald Duck (circa 1920–40) which are now right on top of the established collector's totem pole with Little Orphan Annie and Hopalong Cassidy steadily climbing in popularity and price.

"Sesame Street" of television fame is now making its appearance felt. Keep watching on "telly" and in stores.

It is good judgment for collectors to depend upon leading toy manufacturers, and a few names to keep in mind are: Chein Playthings, Creative Playthings, Ideal Toy Company, Mattel, Inc., Knickerbocker Toy Company, Educational Toys, Inc. (Subsidiary of Topper Corporation). One of the oldest retailers is F. A. O. Schwarz (New York), established in 1862. Their Collectors Corner is worth visiting in order to see, admire and examine the toys of yesterday; and in this way, you can determine for yourself the reason toys are such important collectibles. Rappaport's Toy Bazaar (New York) is also a well-recognized retail store in the east. Colonial Williamsburg has several interesting items in this category, and since this famous restoration links the past with the present, we feel their dolls, toys and games have a collectible future. This should start you thinking about toys of today and deciding on the ones to collect which will become the antiques of tomorrow.

If anyone should ask us to play the role of "Nostradamus" and predict the potentiality of collecting toys, we would, without hesitation reply: "Great!" Toys have always been with us, and always will be. Many books have been written on the subject, and the most positive proof of all is that leading museums around the world have toy collections. By all means, visit a museum with the thought of "toys" on your mind.

In essence, there have been no changes in toys since the early Egyptian and Greek days, but enormous advances have been made in their design, manufacture and materials.

CHAPTER IX

MEDALLIC ART

COMMEMORATIVE MEDALS, TOKENS AND NON-MONETARY COINS

Numismatics (coins and medals) and philately (stamps) are considered the two leading acquisitive interests in the collecting world. Coins are among the oldest collectibles; medals of actual achievement go back to the Roman Empire or earlier; and stamps, as we know them today with adhesive backs, revert no farther back in age than the early 1800s. Both are highly specialized subjects, but numismatics has a multitude of many new, interesting and varied facets for today's collector to explore.

Medallic art—medals, tokens and non-monetary coins, commemorating important events, great achievements, famous people and historic phenomena—has recently attained important rank in numismatica. These commemoratives, in the vernacular of collectors and dealers, are often referred to as "so-called dollars" because of their silver-dollar or near-silver-dollar size.

Since man's discovery of gold and silver, these precious metals have always been used for jewelry and decorative objects. Figuratively, gold and silver speak a universal language. Rarity established their employment as coins of the realm and media of foreign exchange.

Collecting in the field of medallic art also includes very expensive platinum; bronze and other metals. It has fascinating appeal for everyone. Great moments of history come alive, and important achievements and personages are perpetually honored in the exquisite, detailed engravings by distinguished artists. Whether an individual is prompted to collect through his own personal interest in history or art, each will have an intrinsic investment in precious metals and valuable heirlooms.

Among friends and acquaintances around us and from what we read there is tremendous interest in the items produced by The Franklin Mint (Franklin Center, Pennsylvania). Our own admiration and enthusiasm for the specimens which we have observed in sterling silver, platinum and other fine metals led us to seek our research information from William F. Krieg, Vice-President, Collector Service, The Franklin Mint. He has been extremely helpful and we eagerly pass along to you the knowledge we have gathered.

The Franklin Mint is the largest private mint in the world and was founded in 1964. It is a publicly owned corporation with headquarters in America and subsidiaries in Canada and Europe, and is not affiliated with the

United States Mint or any other governmental agency. The company's common stock is traded on the American Stock Exchange and total shares are well over two million. As we are dealing in gold and silver in this chapter, we feel this information will be of especial interest to the investment-minded man or woman. In addition to the collectors' series of coins, tokens and commemorative medals, Franklin Mint also strikes coin of the realm for foreign governments. The first four countries were Tunisia, Panama, the Bahamas and Jamaica. They have recently struck coinage for Trinidad and Tobago.

Your best introduction to the extensive offerings of Franklin Mint is their catalogue, *Numismatic Issues of The Franklin Mint 1971 Edition,* available through leading coin dealers or directly from The Franklin Mint.

We would like to point out to you that the catalogue, over three hundred pages and copiously illustrated, does not include prices. The major portion of the illustrated issues are of limited edition, predetermined through advance subscriptions by Franklin Mint collectors and those who wish to become subscribers. Therefore, we feel it is important to have a copy of *Franklin Mint Issues—Identifications and Valuations,* independently published by Regent Graphics, Ltd., 101 Mohawk Avenue, Scotia, New York 12302.

Prices, you will discover, for both purchase and resale are determined not only by supply and demand, but on the vital factors of: metal content, topical interest, size of the item, artistry of design and reputation of the engraver.

During the short span of its existence, The Franklin

Mint has to its credit hundreds and hundreds of magnificent pieces. Here is a cursory glance:

Commemorative Series struck for: National Commemorative Society (including coin-medals for Apollo 8 Moon Flight, Apollo 11 Moon Landing—net mintage of both, 5,252, sterling silver, offered at $7.25 and now valued around $22); *Société Commémorative des Femmes Célèbres* (honoring great women of history). It is interesting to note that among these many fine medals the Maria Montessori coin-medal in honor of the famous Montessori method of teaching was priced at $7.25 when issued in 1969 and now priced at $15 (mintage 3,223). Amelia Earhart coin-medal (3,220 struck) was introduced at $6.60 and up to $19. And, the commemorative series list continues and includes: the "American Negro Commemorative Society" (Dr. Martin Luther King, Jr., Medal, sterling silver, 1968, mintage 1,379 issued at $7.50 and risen in price to $75); "Catholic Commemorative Medal Society" (Pope John XXIII, 1895, in sterling silver, issued $7.45, up to $27.50 and gaining); *Judaic Heritage Society* (founded in 1969, issues between 1300–1850, sterling silver $9.50 and already values up to around $15); others in the series are: "Medical Heritage Society," "Britannia Commemorative Society," "International Fraternal Commemorative Society," "Texas Under Six Flags" series, the "Life of Christ" series, "Spacecraft Medal" series, "Nation's Monuments" series, the "Gannon Collections" series (tributes to progress in modern American aviation). And, The Franklin Mint's own series: "Presidential, History of the United States," "Antique Car," "States of the Union," "Landmarks of America."

For the collectors of gaming tokens, admission tokens

and transportation tokens, The Franklin Mint offers a stupendous variety. Gaming tokens from five dollars to fifty cents bear the distinguished names of Fabulous Flagler Dog Track, Golden Nugget, Desert Inn, Harold's Club, Paradise Island Casino, Aruba Caribbean Hotel, and many more. These were all minted for the individual casinos but gaming tokens were discontinued at the end of 1969. The series is complete with 267 types (1965–69) and they are almost as difficult as "hen's teeth" to find on the market.

In 1967 The Franklin Mint was selected by the Frontier Village (amusement park in San Jose, California) to mint admission tokens, and in the same year began the minting of transportation tokens. Darby, Pennsylvania, uses Franklin Mint tokens in large quantities and they serve as payment for bus travel, bridge tolls, parking and telephone stations. Twenty-five thousand were issued at $.05 and worth from $.10 to $.25 depending upon the condition (the majority of them have undoubtedly had a lot of hard usage).

The more absorbed you become with the offerings of The Franklin Mint, you will want to investigate the Special Private Issues (United Air Lines, Westinghouse Credit Corporation, the American Legion, Boy Scouts of America and over a hundred others).

Promotional issues (for premiums of "game" coins for advertising purposes) are: Mr. President Game, Famous Facts and Faces Game, Antique Car Coin Game, Landmarks of America Game. We recall the Mr. President Game in 1968 which was promoted by the Shell Oil Company, and we traveled miles out of our way to purchase gasoline at different Shell stations in the hope of receiving a coin marked "Instant Winner." Even though we didn't win, it was great fun; but wish we had been bright enough at the time to save the coins as collectibles.

Now, we are up to zodiac art, a great Franklin Mint innovation. This is the work of Gilroy Roberts, the dean of American medallic sculptors, who is best known for his Kennedy portrait on the U.S. half dollar which has become the most popular coin in the world. He has also designed coins for six foreign countries and medals honoring Dwight D. Eisenhower, Lyndon B. Johnson and Winston Churchill. He spent several years designing and sculpturing his interpretation of the twelve signs of the zodiac. They are collectors' delights and each medal-coin bears Gilroy Roberts' personal initials on both the obverse (head or date side) and reverse (opposite side) as they appear on the Kennedy half dollar. A complete set of twelve (in sterling silver) was issued at $47.50 and valuation is now from $65 to $80.

Franklin Mint's Father's Day ingot, 1971, Christmas ornament issues and fine-art plaques come under the chapter "Silver." There is a Franklin Mint Collectors Society which issues a monthly magazine the *Franklin Mint Almanac*.

MEDALLIC ART COMPANY

Each time you look at the rim of a medal and read the edge lettering MEDALLIC ART CO NY, you have a beautiful collector's piece in your hands. This seventy-year-old firm was founded by two Frenchmen, Henri and Felix Weil, and grew to prominence under the direction of Clyde C. Trees. Today the company is managed by his nephew,

William Trees Louth, a man dedicated to art, numismatics and to medal collecting. He is a life member of the American Numismatic Association and was instrumental in developing many of the medallic art medal series including the "Hall of Fame," "Presidential Art," "Chase Commemorative"—all of which his firm manufactures—and has aided in many ways the Society of Medalists. Medallic Art Company has worked with the most famous American sculptors: Augustus Saint-Gaudens, James Earle Fraser, Victor D. Brenner, Malvina Hoffman, Laura Gardin Fraser, Herbert Adams, Chester Beach, Robert I. Aitken and many others. We have been told that the Medallic Art Company will shortly be moving to Danbury, Connecticut—leaving New York City after almost three quarters of a century.

THE DANBURY MINT

A division of Glendinning Companies, Inc., the Danbury Mint (Westport, Connecticut) creates beautiful art medals honoring great historic events. It does not produce medals nor is it affiliated with the U. S. Mint or any other U. S. Government agency. The medals are struck for this firm by leading private mints. Men in Space is a special mint edition (struck by the famed mint, Birmingham, Ltd. of England) of twenty-one commemorative medals in sterling silver or solid bronze which will preserve forever in beautiful medallic art America's first twenty-one historic space achievements—from the foremost U.S. manned space mission to the unforgettable, triumphant moon landing by Apollo 11. Medals in sterling silver issued at $7.00 and solid bronze $3.50. Actual medals measure 36mm. in diameter which is approximately the size of a U.S. silver dollar. The initial sets of the proof edition were reserved for our courageous astronauts and for President Nixon.

UNITED NATIONS ASSOCIATION OF THE UNITED STATES OF AMERICA

The U.N.A.-U.S.A. Commemorative Medal Program for 1971 struck its first issue in solid sterling silver and issued on the same day as the official United Nations stamp commemorating the same subject. Five subjects were issued in 1971 and the quantity of medals for each commemoration was limited to 10 per cent of the number of stamps circulated. The official price for a collector's cachet—combining medal and stamp was $12.50.

The first issue honors one of the most important milestones of United Nations progress—the recent agreement by the great powers to co-operate in the peaceful development of the seabed and ocean floor, under United Nations auspices, for the benefit of all mankind. The other four medals pay tribute to International Support for Refugees, the World Food Programme, the Universal Postal Union and Elimination of Racial Discrimination.

One does not have to be a collector of medallic art to appreciate these U.N.A.-U.S.A. commemorative medals. The United States of America will celebrate its Bicentennial in 1976, and the United Nations began its second quarter century in 1971. There is nothing more that we can say than that these medals are truly an inspiration in fostering our strongest hope for world-wide peace.

INTERNATIONAL MINT (Washington, D.C.)

"A Nation of Riflemen," a unique, commemorative series of coin-medals in solid platinum, palladium* and silver (executed by the International Mint), has been issued by the National Rifle Association to commemorate our country's Bicentennial in 1976 and the NRA's one hundredth birthday (1971).

The "A Nation of Riflemen" series began in 1971 with the issuance in groups of three every six months through September 1975. The price for each medal, $1,000 for platinum, $125 for palladium and $12 for fine silver, has been guaranteed for the complete set of thirty medals, regardless of increases in the prices of precious metals during the coming years.

The creators of these coin-medals are: Donald Struhar, designer of commemorative art for U.S. service academies (West Point, Annapolis, Air Force, Coast Guard, Merchant Marine); Philip Kraczkowski, renowned sculptor and medalist whose work includes busts of J. Edgar Hoover and Lowell Thomas.

Narratives accompanying each coin-medal are by: L. R. (Bob) Wallack, author of *The Anatomy of Firearms.*

Before the International Mint struck these coin-medals, issued by the NRA, the subjects were carefully selected by an Advisory Board of experts.

This will start you on the road to collecting medallic art. Your excitement in this study really comes when you discover for yourself new mints, new issues, new subjects.

---

* Rare, lustrous, silver-white metal approximately equivalent in value to 24-carat gold.

The *Numismatist* (official publication of the American Numismatic Association) is an excellent publication for keeping up-to-date on medallic art. You may even wish to join the American Numismatic Association, 818 North Cascade Avenue, Colorado Springs, which was founded in 1891 and has around 27,000 members from every state in the union and other countries.

CHAPTER X

SILVER

To speak of silver and say that "It is worth its weight in gold" may seem incongruous, but as we all are aware there has existed for some time a scarcity in the precious-metals market. Rarity, therefore, presents excellent reasons for collecting.

It appeared to have happened overnight that silver dimes, quarters and half dollars underwent radical changes under the Coinage Act of 1965. Since that year these denominations have been "clad" which means they have outer layers bonded to an inner core of other metals for the purpose of either eliminating or reducing the silver content. The silver dollar which was discontinued after 1953 did, however, make an auspicious return in 1971 with the silver edition of the Eisenhower dollar. History tells us that silver has suffered shortages before, and as far back as the reign of Edward III of England the issue of silver pennies was banned due to deficiency of the metal.

Silversmithing is one of the truly great arts and was in the height of its glory in colonial days. It still flourishes, but faces innumerable obstacles:

(1) Difficulty in obtaining this precious white metal.
(2) Exorbitant cost of material and labor.
(3) Fewer dedicated craftsmen engaged in this medium.
(4) Abated consumer interest and demand brought about by the popularity of pewter and stainless steel.

Beautiful works in silver, however, are being produced today by world-famous firms and individual craftsmen who have the same reverence for their profession as the artisans of the past. The standards are high, and the designs simple, classic and timeless. Each period in art has its own expression of form and we feel that whatever relates to good taste has permanent value. Especially in silversmithing, it is interesting to observe how artisans are linking the inspired designs of the past to contemporary translations which will always be recognized as symbolic of the late twentieth century.

It is not likely that the scarcity of silver will ever lead to complete disappearance, but silver items today are not as plentiful as in the past. The gratifying exception is table silver which we hope will always continue to be a cherished tradition with young brides. The antique market is flooded with heavy, decorative Victorian silver which in its ornateness reflects the pomposity of the period, and it is a most sought after collectible.

Collecting today's silver creations is somewhat narrow in scope; primarily confined to silverware, vases, dishes, jewelry and small objects for decoration. Collectors of antiquities have an edge on us as many silver items in their category are only names to us—silver napkin rings (the napkin ring is returning. See chapter on "Miscellanea"), horse brasses of silver, silver tankards, silver gorgets, silver snuffboxes, silver shoehorns and buttonhooks, silver matchboxes, silver shaving mugs and others of a similar nature.

Silver has and always will have unrivaled worth: perpetual intrinsic value; indestructibility; eternal luster and beauty when given proper and loving care. Collect with discernment and select what appeals to you in quality and rarity. Place utmost confidence in recognized reputations of established manufacturers and stores specializing in silver. The list is long and dependable and there are many more names than these few: Tiffany & Co.; the Gorham Company; Samuel Kirk & Son, Inc.; Georg Jensen, Inc.; Reed & Barton Silversmiths; Svend Jensen; International Silver Company; Towle. Do not let the unknown craftsman working quietly in a small studio escape your attention. If you admire his work for its quality and originality, by all means purchase it. In many instances, collectors acquire at reasonable cost the work of an artist who one day may rise to fame. It is well to recall that Paul Revere's genius in silversmithing was of no less importance than his heroic midnight ride during the American Revolution.

Hallmarks are of the same significance as they were in

early days. When the silver of today becomes the antique of tomorrow, the hallmarks will serve as fairly accurate identification of the maker and most likely the date.

Our suggestion on silver collectibles is to let your imagination run along creative lines. If you search for the rare and unusual, you will discover some very worthwhile items. We have admired the sterling silver rabbit paperweights exclusive with Tiffany & Company, around $100. Paperweights are usually associated with glass and are quite rare in silver. They are excellent additions to both paperweight and silver collections. Pillboxes are very much in vogue and accessories of this kind will exemplify the dependence our age has placed on vitamins, aspirin and a variety of pellets including "the Pill." They come in every shape from a book, snail shell, clamshell, turtle, heart to very modern ones with plastic drawers. The ones with plastic drawers should not be ignored, as they combine the old (silver) with the new (plastic— twentieth-century substance).

Silver cigarette boxes and cases should be given due consideration. Many antique collectors specialize in snuffboxes, and, who knows, perhaps some day cigarette smoking may go out with snuff. Cigar and pipe smoking will undoubtedly continue and the tobacco industry has little to fear; at least most of the leaders in the field have already diversified into other areas of business. Silver compacts are interesting and could easily become outmoded if someone invented a facial spray so a woman could powder her face in the morning and it would last all day. Wild imagination? That is exactly what is required of the creative collector. Gorham is thinking along novel, creative lines with—would you believe it—a sterling silver Yo-

Yo which really works! No collector will have everything until this piece is included. Around $12.

Recently in a Chinese restaurant we saw a young couple enjoying chow mein with silver chopsticks. We asked the waiter if silver chopsticks were the custom of the house and he replied, "No. We don't use chopsticks any more, but many people bring their own and in nice little cases." The use of chopsticks is fast disappearing and these silver ones seem like a good collectible. Stieff's sterling decanter labels will have a story to tell future generations of what we are drinking today: Bourbon, gin, scotch, rum, rye, vodka. At least historians can report how open-minded we were on the subject in contrast to the colonial custom of hiding liquor in the so-called "deacon's cabinet."

Our collector's list goes on to silver mugs, marriage cups, trays and trophy awards of which there are many beautiful ones around today. Animal sculptures and figurines are not aplenty, but there are indeed many interesting ones.

We have covered commemorative spoons, medallic art (medals and non-monetary coins) in special chapters. However, regarding issues of The Franklin Mint, we have saved for this chapter where they rightfully belong:

(1) A series of solid sterling Christmas plates designed by Norman Rockwell and his first work in this medium. The first plate was issued in 1970 entitled Bringing Home the Tree. Limited edition of 18,000 at $100. It is now reported by dealers in the $400–$500 range. The 1971 issue is entitled Under the Mistletoe and there will be four more to follow.

(2) 1971 Mother's Day commemoratives—solid sterling silver-proof medal at $9.50; solid 18-carat gold pendant-charm at $75; 24-carat gold on sterling pendant charm at $12.50; and solid sterling silver pendant charm at $7.50—available to members of The Franklin Mint Collectors Society only.

(3) 1971 Father's Day Ingot in solid sterling silver at $12.50. Available to members of The Franklin Mint Collectors Society exclusively.

(4) "Christmas Ornament" series. Twelve designs illustrating the Twelve Days of Christmas. These are of nickel-silver inserted in lucite. The first edition 1966 was around 2,500 net mintage and now valued by dealers (when available) at $45. In 1970 new editions of this series in platinum, sterling silver and bronze were introduced.

(5) Fine Art Plaques are masterpieces in sculptured art by outstanding artists. Issued in exceptionally limited editions and mounted for wall display, their values have increased greatly whenever available from collectors or at auctions. John F. Kennedy by Gilroy Roberts was issued in 1967 in a limited edition of 50 at $750 and now valued at $1,800. Others in the series by Gilroy Roberts are Horses issued in 1968 limited to an edition of 250 at $350 and now valued at $1,000 and Wild Geese, 1969, limited to an edition of 50 at $750 and now listed at $1,450. Other artists represented include: Paul Vincze, Alex Hromych, Umberto Romano, Charles Parks and Carlos Sierra-Franco. To keep *au courant* on subsequent issues in this series, we recommend that you contact The Franklin Mint,

Collector Services, Franklin Center, Pennsylvania 19063. In this manner you will be apprised of what is forthcoming and be able to purchase each new piece as a subscriber and not lose out in either time or money waiting until the plaque you most desire reaches a dealer which is seldom.

We hope that your journey into the collection of modern silver will prove fascinating and profitable.

CHAPTER XI

PLAYING CARDS AND GAMES

PLAYING CARDS

Interesting collectibles are right in the palms of your hands each time you spend pleasurable hours playing bridge, poker, gin and other popular card games. The collecting of playing cards is growing fast with thousands of collectors all over the world, many of whom have formed their own clubs. Yet, it is amazing what little importance most of us give to playing cards except as vehicles of relaxation and fun. The historic significance of card faces and the intriguing artistic designs on the backs are usually ignored by most people whose sole intent is to win a grand slam or pick up the chips.

The history of playing cards has been traced back to ancient Egypt, age-old China and prehistoric India. They were hand-painted on wood, ivory, dried leaves, tiles and a variety of other materials until the invention of the printing press. Among the many speculations on how and why playing cards were invented and the purposes for which they were used are that Tarot cards (of which there is a great interest and revival today) were designed for prophetic divination and not for amusement. It has been acceptably established by experts that the Crusaders found playing cards in the Orient and used them for gambling games. Then they were introduced into Europe, possibly by the gypsies for fortunetelling.

In the fourteenth century the first pack of cards similar to the ones we use today was designed. It was an ingenious and precise mathematical invention. Take a pack of cards and you will see:

> 52 cards in the deck (one for each week of the year)
> 365 spots (representing the days of the year)
> 4 suits—Hearts (clergy)
>   Spades (spikes—soldiers)
>   Diamonds (artisans)
>   Clubs (clover—land)
> 13 cards to a suit (one for each month, reckoned by the Julian calendar)
> Ten numerals—Ace (1) to 10
> King, queen, jack (picture cards, formerly called court cards)

Suits, as you will note, are red and black. The reason for these two colors is not actually known, but there are two thoughts: (1) influence of chessboards or (2) Piquet —the earliest game known to be played with cards. In medieval days the colors red and black had the great significance of symbolizing the military and the clergy. The "joker" came late in the life of playing cards, and

experts have not as yet determined its origin. One specu-
lation is that an extra card was needed for certain games.

The story of playing cards embraces every scope of human studies—history, religion, politics, art and archaeol-
ogy. Old playing cards are on exhibit in many famous
museums around the world and in private collections.
The most complete collection in this country which we
have heard about is The United States Playing Card Collection on permanent loan to the Cincinnati Art Museum.
Exploration of this subject has brought us into communication with The United States Playing Card Company
from whom we have received valuable assistance and information.

Our first recommendation to every neophyte in this
line of collecting is to become acquainted with the
monthly feature, "Playing Cards," conducted by Dorothy
Powills in *Hobbies*. This has been a regular *Hobbies'* department since 1939 and Mrs. Powills has been editor
since 1962 as well as writing most of the articles. For the
Encylopedia Americana she has written "Cards, Playing," a concise, condensed review of the subject with mention of collections and collecting. We would like very
much to see *Hobbies* publish its own encyclopedia
of playing cards, incorporating all of the articles on the
subject which have appeared in the magazine. This would
most certainly stir up enormous interest in this fascinating
hobby which is inexpensive, artistic, educational and
requires the minimum of space in contrast to the majority
of collectibles. Collecting of single card backs is the most
prevalent procedure except in the most unusual circumstances of desiring complete and full decks. Decorative
card backs are comparatively recent, as the early cards

had plain white backs, which had many uses in olden days as invitations, visiting cards, admission cards and money during a national emergency. In the 1800s decorative backs came into vogue and designs have been of every conceivable nature—portraits, flowers, animals, historic scenes, travel, paintings of old masters, etc. Railroads, steamship lines, hotels, inns, restaurants, tobacco companies and other businesses were quick to recognize a new advertising medium and issued their own decks of playing cards.

The lore of playing cards holds untold interest for historians and romanticists. As you delve into the study, you will come across significant historic and social references to playing cards: how a deck was designed to promulgate the plot to assassinate a king; the general who was so engrossed in his game of cards that he failed to read an urgent message and lost the battle and his life; a proletarian deck of cards which maligned the royalty; the slick method of recruiting sailors (money to the few winners and a long sea voyage to the many losers); a scheming bride who was an expert cardplayer and ended her marriage on her wedding night when the groom lost the game and his bride; and the court physicians, long before the days of psychiatry, who hit upon the therapy of soothing the mind of a mad king by encouraging him to play cards day and night.

The real old playing cards are scarce, and valuations, as far as we can ascertain, seem to be enshrouded in mystery. Mainly because the rare ones are in the possession of museums and the relatively few in private collections seldom appear on the dealer or auction markets. It has been reported that back in 1392 when Jacquemin

Gringonneur, the French painter, designed his playing cards, the royal ledger at the time made an entry for three sets at a sum which in today's equivalent would be around $500. Possibly even more!

In the United States the collecting of playing cards began around the turn of the century and decks prior to this period are considered antiques. As collecting is still not acknowledgeably widespread, we feel that this is the most opportune time to start assembling modern playing cards and get on the bandwagon of possibly the *newest of the new collectibles.*

The playing cards manufactured today are magnificent in design and subject. As a beginner, it is acceptable to assemble the cards which interest you the most. After you have acquired a variety and become interested in the study of cards, you will automatically divert to specialized categories and consequently develop an unusual collection.

Among the playing cards we would bet on for becoming tomorrow's antiques are:

Space Age: Almost anything at all in this category. NASA (National Aeronautics and Space Administration) should head the list. The United States Playing Card Company launched its standard Bicycle playing cards (on fireproof paper) on a recent Apollo moon landing. Initial production was a mere several hundred packs, and happy are the collectors who have been fortunate enough to possess one deck. These same NASA cards should be appearing in the near future on the consumer market.

Railroads: Train schedules are running behind, but this is an important, and somewhat limited, category in the collecting of playing cards. For years the cards found in club cars, parlor cars and the staterooms of Pullman cars have been desirable collectibles. Don't delay or stop over in collecting them today. They are still vital memorabilia of Americana—depicting on the backs famous names in railroading, or scenic illustrations of America from coast to coast. Please, though, under no condition appropriate them—tip the porter well and he will give them to you with a big, broad Redcap smile.

Steamships: In this category, the whistles blow "All Aboard" for collecting. The tides of time are getting low, especially for transatlantic travel. Look around now in the secondhand stores and in dealer's shops for playing cards from the United States Lines, Cunard Line, French Line and all the others.

Air Travel: A smooth flight for the collector! And, keep in mind anything as new as "747."

Presidents of the United States: Presidential card collecting is a field of its own. George Washington and other early Presidents have long been featured on the backs of playing cards. Keep an eagle's eye open for the new issues honoring these men as they are bound to appear from time to time in new designs, poses or scenes associated with their lives. Start your collecting for tomorrow's antiquities with:

Franklin Delano Roosevelt—comparatively few but there are two good decks showing his home at Hyde

Park and his little White House in Warm Springs, Georgia.

Dwight David Eisenhower—there is one back design of the Eisenhower Museum at Abilene, Kansas. Several political designs during his campaigns: "I Like Ike" and "We Still Like Ike." Most unusual and very scarce is the limited edition of Eisenhower's oil paintings of George Washington and Abraham Lincoln.

John F. Kennedy—The memorial issue with the bust of President Kennedy is valuable.

Lyndon Baines Johnson—LBJ's Texas White House is illustrated on a pack of cards issued during his term as President. Also several political campaign decks.

American Bicentennial (1776–1976): Hear Ye! Hear Ye! The Grand Slam (named after the victorious Battle of Trenton, the turning point of the War of Independence) Bridge Set is a limited edition of 2,400 numbered sets, for the 2,400 ragged and freezing men who crossed the icy Delaware River with Washington on the night of December 25, 1776. Sets are priced at $35 and truly a great collector's find.

Our list continues on to Tarot Cards which are all the rage today. We confess that we don't know how to tell fortunes, but there is a good book *Tarot Cards for Fun and Fortune Telling* which describes the meaning of each card. Round playing cards, a novelty of the nineteenth century, are back on the market and interesting collectibles along with midget and giant cards. The autograph cards of famous people are intriguing. From time to time you will also find limited editions of playing cards issued by leading organizations to celebrate an anniversary, or for other promotional reasons. For elegance that can't be surpassed, there are plain or monogrammed decks with beautifully designed spot sides and the imposing words "Tiffany & Co., New York."

Clubs for Collectors: Chicago Playing Card Collectors, Inc. (9645 South Leavitt St., Chicago, Illinois 60643) was founded in the 1950s and is under the directorship of Mrs. Dorothy Powills; and Playing Cards Collectors' Association, Inc. (Sturgeon Bay, Wisconsin 54235). They both invite membership inquiries. Among the books on the subject are: *Old and Curious Playing Cards, Their History and Types from Many Countries and Periods,* by H. T. Morley; *The History of Playing Cards,* by E. S. Taylor; and highly recommended *The American Card Catalog—The Standard Guide on All Collected Cards and Their Values* (Kistler Printing Company, East Stroudsburg, Pennsylvania). This volume includes all forms of cards: advertising, souvenir, insert, premium and greeting. Who knows, one thing may lead to another!

Games: New games come and go, but the old-time favorites stay on forever in new designs and new guises. These are the issues to collect.

As an example Monopoly (Parker Brothers) is thirty-seven years old and still a best-selling board game. We were told that more Monopoly games were sold in 1970 than in any previous year. Of interest to collectors are the changes in packaging and up-dating. When new editions are introduced the old ones are dropped. In Monopoly, for example, houses and hotels have been changed from wood to plastic and the $25 deluxe edition in a wooden case has been discontinued in favor of a $20 deluxe edition in a plastic carrying case.

The card games such as pit, rook, and rummy are old household words, but they often come out in new packaging and look younger. Collectors want them. Browse through the game departments in stores and your choice will be as good as anyone else's. Don't miss Masterpiece, the Art Auction Game. Fortunately, it is a Parker Brothers production as already it has been called "the best game since Monopoly." Scrabble, backgammon, parcheesi are good collectibles.

Action games, space games, military games, travel games, and all the other fast-moving games are definitely late twentieth-century collectibles with a future. Many game collectors won't move to any other category but Jigsaw Puzzles. If you, too, are so inclined, be choosy and select the subject matter of the puzzle with care. Topical interest should be a winner with the Norman Rockwell puzzles from his famous *Saturday Evening Post* covers; or the New York *Times* puzzles; actual reproductions of historic front pages including astronaut Alan Shephard's flight in space; and the war between Israel and the Arab nations. The latest of all are the Photo Jigsaws. We became acquainted with them last Christmas when we saw an advertisement in the mail-order pages of *National Observer*. We answered the advertisement and sent some photographs of family, friends, pets, houses and had them made into Jigsaw Puzzles. The cost was nominal (about $5.00 each), and they made great, inexpensive gifts. Items such as this are definitely collectibles.

Name your game. Buy one to play and enjoy and one to add to your collection. Sounds like good fun for every one!

CHAPTER XII

GLASS

When the supposed apple fell from the tree and hit Sir Isaac Newton on the head (whether truth or fiction we do not know), he discovered the Law of Gravity. Glass, attributed to the Phoenicians, came into our lives in a fortuitous manner. The familiar story which has been circulated concerns the wandering merchants who stopped along the shores of the sea to rest and eat their midday meal. Soon after they had placed their cooking vessels on blocks of natron (subcarbonate of soda), they were overwhelmed by an amazing sight. A strange, new substance was produced by the heat of the alkali and sand. It was the formula for glassmaking, one of the greatest crafts the world has ever known. Fortunately, this band of merchants were good businessmen and quick to realize that they had come upon a most unusual discovery. They decided to share this great secret with

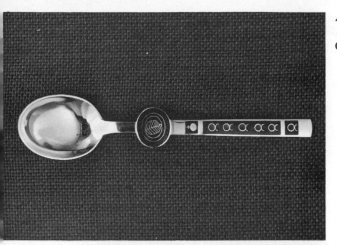

48. Spoon of the Month (May) by A. Michelsen, Copenhagen.

49. Lafayette Paperweight by Baccarat Crystal.

50. Will Rogers Paperweight by Baccarat Crystal.

51. Custom-made
Carousel Music Boxes
by Rita Ford, Inc.

52. Stephen Foster
Music Box
by Rita Ford, Inc.

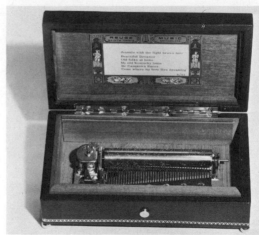

53. "Snoopy in Space," Musical
Toy, courtesy G. Schirmer, Inc.,
photo by Schmid Brothers, Inc.

1260 NORTH WETHERLY DRIVE

HOLLYWOOD 46, CALIFORNIA

November 12, 1953
Air Mail

Mr Philip Wittenberg
Attorney
70 West 40th Street
New York, N.Y.

Dear Mr Wittenberg,

Following the shocking news of Dylan Thomas' sudden
passing away, I have read in the New York Times that
you are the Treasurer of a Fund organized to give
assistance to the Thomas family.

Incidentally let me say that I consider this initiative
as a most appropriate one and I hope it will meet with
the active support of all the friends and admirers of
the deceased.

Being myself one of Dylan Thomas' great admirers I
beg you to put into this fund the enclosed check as my
personal contribtion.

Having been deprived to meet Mrs Thomas, I would appreciate
your being instrumental in forwarding to her the expression
of my deepest and sincerest sympathy.

Yours truly,

Igor Stravinsky

Encl.

54. Igor Stravinsky Autograph Letter,
courtesy Walter R. Benjamin Autographs, Inc.

13th March, 1918.

My dear Samuel,

This is just to acknowledge the receipt
of your letter of to-day on the subject of the
scheme for the recovery of potash from blast furnace
dust.   I will look into the matter and write to
you again on the subject in the course of a day
or two.

Yours sincerely,

Winston S. Churchill

The Right Hon. Herbert Samuel, M.P.,
    31, Porchester Terrace,
        Hyde Park,
            W.2.

55. Winston Churchill
Autograph Letter,
courtesy Walter R. Benjamin
Autographs, Inc.

56. (RIGHT) Beam
"Bing Crosby" Bottle,
James B. Beam
Distilling Co.

57. (FAR RIGHT) Beam
1968 Executive
"Presidential" Bottle,
James B. Beam
Distilling Co.

58. Ezra Brooks
"Rooster" Bottle.

59. Ezra Brooks
"Silver Spur" Bottle.

60. Figural by Lionstone Distilleries, Ltd.,
photo by Birlauf & Steen, Inc.

61. Figural by Lionstone
Distilleries, Ltd.,
photo by Birlauf & Steen, Inc.

62. American Patriot Series
by Frankfort Distilling Co., photo by
Milton Fenster Associates Inc.

63. Zodiac Series by Frankfort
Distilling Co., photo by Milton Fenster
Associates Inc.

64. Sabra Liqueur Pilgrim Flask, courtesy Park Avenue Imports.

65. Old Cars Series by Double Springs Distillers, Inc.

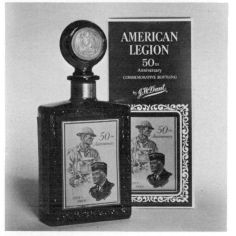

66. J. W. Dant American Legion Commemorative Bottle, Schenley Industries, Inc.

67. J. W. Dant Boeing 747 Bottle,
Schenley Industries, Inc.

68. J. W. Dant Fort Sill Centennial
Bottle, Schenley Industries, Inc.

69. Coca-Cola Bottles 1894–1970,
courtesy Archives Coca-Cola USA,
photo by Leviton, Atlanta.

chemists and ceramic artists and thereby create a new line of merchandise for themselves.

Other ancient people practiced glassmaking from a very early period, and the oldest examples, of which dates are attested by inscriptions, are of Egyptian origin. After the fall of the Roman Empire, however, the manufacture of glass subsided somewhat until the craft was revived in Venice in the eleventh century and then soon spread throughout Europe. The Venetian island of Murano became the great center for celebrated glasshouses where its fame still flourishes today. When America was discovered, no trace of glass was in existence, but it eventually made its appearance in this country with the colonists at the beginning of the seventeenth century.

Glass is one of the most beautiful objects to collect, certainly the most fragile and delicate; and it has come to mean many things to many people. Good glass is brilliant and sparkling, elegant, artistic and ageless. Most remarkable of all is that glass is always glad and never sad (unless it needs a washing). It has been explained to us that glassblowers are truly happy people and their work is a step-by-step dance expressing their talents in lyrical movements. As romanticists and poets, we suppose that they envision how their goblets and plates will look on a banquet table; how flowers will be arranged in vases; what kind of libations will be poured from the bottles and all the important letters (and bills) which will be protected by paperweights.

We have introduced you to glass in our chapters on paperweights and bottles. Now, we will journey into other glass acquisitions with our recommendations on present-day glass which we consider worthy collectibles.

STEUBEN GLASS (U.S.A.)

With a collection of Steuben Glass you are in the company of famous museums around the world where it is proudly exhibited; and, in kindred association with illustrious people who assemble these great works of glass art for their private collections. Any connoisseur of art will apprise you that Steuben Glass does not have to wait the test of time for acclaimed recognition as a most highly regarded and greatly desired collectible.

Steuben Glass, as we know it today, crossed the threshold of fame soon after the firm was established in 1933 under the leadership of Arthur Amory Houghton, Jr., great-grandson of the founder of Corning Glass Works, Corning, New York. The name Steuben came into being in 1903 when Frederick Carder, an English glassmaker, established a factory at Corning, naming it after Steuben County in which Corning is located. In 1918 his business was acquired by Corning Glass Works, and thereafter became the Steuben Division of that company, producing fine handmade glass.

In 1933 when Mr. Houghton, a scholar of the arts, took over the Steuben Division, his aims were a trilogy: *design, quality* and *workmanship*. Now nearly forty years later his dreams have been realized and Steuben ranks among the finest glass ever made. Mr. Houghton has always surrounded himself with talented men who shared his dedication to the art of glassmaking.

Steuben Glass is made at the Corning Glass Center which serves as headquarters for the entire glass world. In addition to the manufactory, the famous Corning Museum of Glass is located there, and its extensive collection is a living record of the history of glass. The Corning Glass Center has a library, fascinating exhibition halls and observation galleries where visitors are offered a firsthand view of the making of glass products; including every step from the blowing to the finishing and engraving operations. Intriguing terms such as "glory hole," "servitor," "the gaffer" and "stick-up boy" are all explained and experiences of this kind are both instructive and fun.

If you are already acquainted with Steuben Glass, then you will actually need no urging on our part to collect it. Each individual piece speaks for itself, and the message it conveys to the eye and touch far outweigh any words of glowing praises we can proffer. Steuben Crystal is sold mainly at Steuben's own shop on Fifth Avenue and Fifty-sixth Street (New York), and at Corning Glass Center (Corning, New York). Visitors at both locations are cordially invited to see the complete collections on display. It is seldom that anyone (never, certainly a collector of glass) leaves either emporium without a purchase. Occasionally you will see ornamental pieces in select shops such as Gump's in San Francisco, Shreve, Crumpet and Low in Boston and other similar establishments. Even the tiniest sculptured piece may eventually become one of the most prized possessions in your collection. As an illustration, the small snail (3¼ inches in length) now retails for $50 and although the snail will never grow, we can foresee its value increasing greatly.

Steuben sculptures are by well-known, recognized artists. George Thompson, on the Steuben staff since 1936, has among his famed creations, The Crown Cup (collection of Queen Elizabeth, the Queen Mother), Cathedral (collection of France's late President Charles de Gaulle). Sidney Waugh, distinguished American sculptor and Steuben's chief associate designer, deserves much of the credit for establishing engraved crystal as an art form. Waugh's designs created such interest that Steuben commissioned leading painters, sculptors and designers all over the world to execute drawings for copper-wheel engravings, and then glass forms faithful to the drawings were translated into beautiful works of glass art. Bruce Moore, an American sculptor known for his animal figures was invited by Steuben to bring his talents to the medium of glass. Don Wier, Donald Pollard, Lloyd Atkins, Pavel Tchelitchew, and James Houston are among the many great designers of Steuben Crystal. To collectors, the union of Steuben and a famous designer is twofold: (1) heirloom piece of Steuben Crystal and (2) masterpiece of design by a renowned artist.

Throughout the world there have been many major exhibitions of Steuben Glass. Public collections include the following museums (and many more): Metropolitan Museum of Art, New York; Victoria and Albert Museum, London; Princeton Museum, New Jersey; Carnegie Institute, Pennsylvania; Toledo Museum of Art, Ohio; City Art Museum of St. Louis, Missouri; Art Institute of Chicago, Illinois; City Art Gallery, Bristol (England). Steuben Crystal has been greatly honored by recognition in many private collections: H.M. King Baudouin I, Belgium, Their Majesties King Frederik IX and Queen Ingrid, Denmark; H.M. King Haakon VII, Norway; H.M. Queen Elizabeth II and H.R.H. The Duke of Edinburgh,

United Kingdom, President Dwight David Eisenhower and Pope Pius XII, Vatican City.

Do take time to examine a few pieces of Steuben Glass carefully. We feel that you will agree with us that there is great pleasure and delight in the imagery expressed in: Ice Bear (James Houston)—a crystal iceberg on whose crest stands a silver polar bear; Crystal and Vermeil Turtle (Paul Schulze)—turtle with cut and polished shell of clear crystal; Hyperbolas (George Thompson)—tall rectangular crystal block cut in two narrow arches, one pointing up and the other down. These creative interpretations of familiar subjects are true glass art, and represent a vast departure from the prosaic glassmaking traditions of decorating functional forms for vases, bowls, glasses and other accessories for everyday use.

Everything signed by the name "Steuben" is a collectible. The glass figurines which Steuben refers to as the "Animal Fair" are a convincing reminder of Noah and a recording of all of his animal, fish and bird friends— whale, alligator, penguin, porpoise, duckling, mouse, cat, elephant, giraffe, owl, pheasant. Name it and you will find it. Noah himself in a majestic tapestry robe of living creatures (glass design by Paul Schulze, sculpture by Frank Eliscu) made a grand appearance in a limited edition of ten at $8,500 each. Always remember, when you are purchasing Steuben pieces, you are collecting masterpieces of art—authoritatively important today in their own right, and destined to become valuable antiques of tomorrow. Once you become fully acquainted with Steuben Glass you will recognize it anywhere. An item which sold for a few dollars twenty-five years ago may be worth hundreds of dollars today. And the pieces you buy today will have greater value tomorrow.

ROYAL LEERDAM (Holland)

We have been told that the first glassmakers in America were "eight Dutchmen and Poles" who landed at Jamestown, Virginia, in 1608. Therefore, it seems most appropriate that this firm of experienced craftsmen in Leerdam, Holland, has been entrusted with the mouth-blown and hand-formed Williamsburg glassware.

Royal Leerdam creates decanters, bottles, jugs and lipped finger bowls (similar to the kind our forefathers used to rinse their wine glasses between servings). It demands great artistry and technical skill to produce fine glassware from fragments excavated in Williamsburg, and from the antiques in the Exhibition Buildings of Colonial Williamsburg. Royal Leerdam is a licensed manufacturer of the Reproductions Program of Colonial Williamsburg. At this point, we would like to mention that Williamsburg reproductions are in truth "re-creations" and not simulations. A simple explanation is that from the earliest days of the restoration (1937), visitors to this historic colonial city have been inspired by the magnificent buildings and their exquisite antique furnishings. Thus, in response to the great enthusiasm of visitors and the desire to have furniture, wallpapers, silver, glass, etc., for their own homes of equal quality and authenticity, Colonial Williamsburg began its program of reproductions. It is not a vast production and items for "re-creation" are selectively chosen and for the most part (as far as we know) sold chiefly through the Craft House in

Williamsburg. We consider these Royal Leerdam pieces of glass worthy collectibles, and this particular line could, just possibly, be discontinued one of these years.

IMPERIAL GLASS (U.S.A.)

This long-established American company (1904) is well named as the glass is excellent, interesting and falls into many collectible categories. In fact, in the collector's world it is much sought after. Miss Lucile J. Kennedy, assistant to the president of Imperial Glass, told us that whenever an item or a line is discontinued, people immediately start asking for it so they can pack it away for the future or add it to a collection. Browse around the shops specializing in glassware and china (a combined section in department stores) and look at Imperial Glass. The prices for the new are current, and the old pieces keep step with the antique market.

Among Imperial's clever, handcrafted unusualities, you will find: "Crystal Coins"—the first-of-a-series plate produced only in 1971. It features in clear crystal the complete 1964 set of United States coins—Kennedy half dollar, Washington quarter, Roosevelt dime, Jefferson nickel and Lincoln penny. Coin collectors will immediately recognize them as the last of the "unclad coins." (From 1964 all coins have been "clad"—our chapter on "Silver" explains this minutely.) This Imperial crystal coin plate retails around $15. For the collectors of glass, it is a *must*, and interesting and novel enough to give to a coin buff. Christmas plates—a limited edition of the first of a series commemorating the "Twelve Days of Christmas" was issued in 1970 with everybody's favorite, A Partridge in a

Pear Tree. 1971 follows with Two Turtle Doves, then Three French Hens in 1972. By 1981 you will have Four Colly Birds, Five Gold Rings, Six Geese A-laying, Seven Swans A-swimming, Eight Maids A-milking, Nine Drummers Drumming, Ten Pipers Piping, Eleven Ladies Dancing and Twelve Lords A-leaping. The twelve days of Christmas preserved forever in beautiful glass plates (as they say at Belmont Race Tracks "to show and win").

ORREFORS (Sweden)

Orrefors is a small, rustic town in Sweden and known the world over for its elegant crystal. The company was founded in 1726 as an ironworks and began a modest production of glassware and window glass in 1898. After World War I, Orrefors concentrated on graal glass with inlaid colors and ariel glass which utilized air bubbles to enhance the designs. Results were so exceptional that in 1925 Orrefors won the *Grand Prix* for engraved glass at the Paris Exposition. Collectors and connoisseurs of fine glass regard Orrefors crystal as "museum pieces." As a neophyte collector, begin your Orrefors with the new series of collector's plates: Notre Dame, 1970 ($45); Westminster Abbey, 1971 ($50). We have mentioned Orrefors under "Paperweights." Good news is that Orrefors may in the immediate future produce limited editions of crystal figurines. Keep an eye out for them.

KASTRUP-HOLMEGAARD (Denmark)

Founded in 1825, this company enjoys the reputation of being the official glassmakers to the king of Denmark. Anything, and everything, you like in this line is collectible. Their animal figurines are charming, and the Astronaut is a winner.

From the Swedish glass factories, Kosta and Boda, you will find unique sculpture, ashtrays, perfume bottles, bowls, vases and other decorative pieces. St. Louis Cristal de France, Baccarat Crystal and Waterford (Ireland) continue to produce elegant work.

Among antique collectors carnival glass is quite the rage, and the Fenton Art Glass is now issuing a series of Carnival Glass annual plates. The first came out in 1970 with the Glassblower.

Most noteworthy is the glass art by Jan Cerny, professor at the School of Sculptors in Czechoslovakia. A series of ten pieces is to be introduced, and the first is the Owl, an edition of two hundred individually signed and numbered. The price is $170. Cerny's work is to be followed with interest as he recently exhibited three pieces at an art exhibition in Paris, and each piece sold for $1,500.

The subject of glass covers a wide and varied field and the best advice to a beginner is: (1) concentrate on one or two specific categories, such as plates, mugs, figurines; (2) place confidence in the old-established manufacturers; (3) don't buy anything unless you truly admire it.

As you browse through antique publications, you will see the importance of glass; and there is every reason to suppose that the glass you collect today will have a very significant place in the world of tomorrow's antiques. Enjoy your glass, display it and use the functional pieces, especially on important occasions.

CHAPTER XIII

BUTTONS

The old expression, "I wouldn't give a button for it," classifies buttons as diminutive items despite their essential usefulness. Up until comparatively recent years, anyone interested in collecting them would have been said "to have lost his buttons." There has always been, of course, a select group of collectors who have assembled buttons for their jewels, fine enameling or the historic importance of having belonged to a famous personage.

The innovation of the zipper has brought buttons more or less into obsolescence and into the hands of collectors. "Button, button, who has the button?" has now become the slogan of an enormous rank and file of collectors. Little wonder! Buttons are small, fascinating collectibles, require little space at home and offer a promising monetary return. Even the most insignificant buttons which sold for around fifteen cents apiece twenty years ago are now often priced from $5.00 to $15, and in particular instances even higher.

Buttons have an interesting history dating back before 2000 B.C. and there is fascinating lore concerning them. In early days buttons were not only used for utilitarian purposes, but to distinguish the common folks from the nobility. As late as the reign of King Henry VIII, an Act of Parliament required peasants to wear buttons of horn and bone; silver, gold and precious stones were reserved for those of noble birth. We read with interest how a button saved Handel's life when he was engaged in a duel. The point of his opponent's sword struck one of the composer's buttons; the sword snapped and Handel was saved to write his great music. Buttons set fashions, too. Once there was a portly king who could not fasten the lower button of his waistcoat, and his subjects, eager to win his favor, copied the style. Decades later, on a windy day, a queen wrapped her coat around her and immediately initiated the sophisticated vogue for women's buttonless coats.

Buttons have become such important collectibles that *Hobbies* has a monthly department entitled, "Button Collecting," conducted by Dorothy Foster Brown who is the author of *Button Parade,* a book that belongs in the library of every button collector along with *The Collector's Encyclopedia of Buttons* by Sally Luscomb. Button collectors have their own clubs and a publication, *National Button Bulletin.* Begin to read everything you can about buttons, and you will be amazed how much there is to learn. There is a National Button Society as well as numerous state and local groups dedicated to the study and collection of buttons.

Buttons come in every conceivable size and shape—round, square, oblong, hexagon and octagon. Every kind of material has been used—wood, wool, cotton, linen, porcelain, leather, pearl and other jewels, bones, gold, silver, copper, brass, pewter, ivory and right up to nylon and other man-made fabrics. Topical interests in designs include birds, fish, animals, flowers, geometric patterns, zodiac signs, emblems and insignia, portraits; and you name all the others.

During the years buttons of historic importance or those made of exquisite jewels and belonging to famous people have been assembled in museums and private collections and many have been placed on auction. Back in the early 1960s a large collection was sold in London at Sotheby's for around $20,000. This attests to the fact that buttons are seriously collected by experts interested in the fields of art, costume design and history. We consider button collecting most important, and look upon today as a most auspicious time to begin.

What to collect? Any type of buttons which appeal to you. There are innumerable varieties:

Sew-on buttons—Men's and women's garments
                Uniforms
                College blazers
                Yachting Clubs
                Railroad and Steamship Lines

Pin buttons—Political, advertising, fraternal, lodges, comics. And, don't miss some of today's crazy Fun Buttons: *I am an official U.S. taxpayer; My heart belongs to you, I've given my brain to science;* and the button with the great, big SMILE.

Butcher buttons—Work clothes and overalls (metal
  shank with bolt or ring which keeps
  the button in place).

Clamp-back buttons—Work clothes (prongs at back
  which are pressed into the gar-
  ment).

However, we would like to point out to you that from
our own business experience, there is tremendous interest
in militaria; uniform buttons are therefore most important
collectibles. There is a wild collecting craze at the present
time for uniforms, insignia, headgear of World War II
with great emphasis on relics of the Axis nations. (See
Firearms and Militaria.) Political campaign buttons are
a specific study. An excellent book on the subject is *Political Campaign Buttons in Color with Prices* by Otha
Wearin. This will acquaint you with presidential campaign buttons (1898–1968), national and state badges,
women's campaign items, independent and third-party
buttons. Identification is clear and the price list is up-to-
date (1970). Another good reference work is *The Illustrated Political Button Book* by Dick Bristow which pictures over 4,000 politicals from 1896 to 1968 and has a
price guide. With the presidential election coming up
this year, now is a good time to get interested in the political buttons. Try for the jugates which show pictures
of both the presidential and vice-presidential candidates.
These sell for greatly higher prices than the single pictures. As an example: COX-FDR jugate (1920) is priced
today on the dealer's market around $1,500; and single
pictures of each candidate $75. FDR-TRUMAN (1944)
—jugate $20 and each single picture $2.00. Kennedy buttons are scarce and when available they are on the high

side. Keep on the lookout—as time goes on they will be appearing on the market. Attics, flea markets and curio shops are good places to search for them.

The button-collecting boom is just commencing. If you like buttons for their history, romance, designs, or any reason at all, collect them. Forget for the present what future cash appreciation will be, as it is much too early to make a prediction.

Buttons are fast becoming "relics of the past," and if you begin collecting now you will have much pleasure and really be assembling the treasures of tomorrow.

CHAPTER XIV

FIREARMS AND MILITARIA

Two of the very large and certainly important fields of collecting are those of firearms and military material. The study is encyclopedic and encompasses world history from its beginning right through to the present day. It includes all of man's warlike endeavors on both land and sea over this entire period.

MODERN COLLECTIBLES

Actually, there are quite a few since World War II. It is surprising to note that in a number of instances certain World War II items have already achieved a great amount of rarity and commensurate high values. It is also amazing to observe that the collectibles which have reached these prices are chiefly from countries which did the most to injure mankind. The Fascist and Axis nations. As a matter of fact, prices on certain items have risen to such an enormous extent—with the popularity of other items constantly growing—that probably more spurious and fake specimens have been made in Germany and Europe since the war than were manufactured during the entire time of the Nazi regime. The collecting fever is so contagious that this is a warning for which the modern-day collector must be on the watch.

It may generally be said that the material of the free and united nations of World War II, especially the United States of America and England, is much less sought after because its availability is in large quantities. It probably is less attractive to the modern-day younger collector because of the less evil-like appearance. There seems to be a built-in horror of satanic wickedness surrounding much of the Nazi and other Fascist material which was designed to capture the imagination of their respective peoples during the actual time they were used, and still continues to do so. Most unusual of all is the strong fascination which the nations who did the most to bring down the Axis powers have for this type of material. America and England are today the largest markets for these morbid souvenirs.

Fortunately, though, modern collectibles in this field cover a varied and wide area. Following is a list of specific areas of collecting, each of which has its own devotees and market. The modern era commences with memorabilia of World War II.

UNIFORMS AND HEADGEAR

For sheer pageantry, color and exhibition purposes this field probably would take honors, although it is certainly not without its drawbacks! A major hazard would be defending it annually against the invasion of the moth! Certain uniforms—again those of the Axis powers —have achieved considerable price rises and are in great demand. Buyers must be wary of fakes and forgeries which are actually being turned out to this day. There are, however, many other peripheral fields which are wide open in which the collector can have great enjoyment and assemble a collection at a very moderate price which should have excellent potentials for the future. The obvious rule of thumb is, of course, those uniforms which are most difficult to obtain, less accessible; and those which will bring the most money in the future. The range covers a wide variety in appearance and rank. For instance, the most handsome of dress uniforms, especially of European army-elite groups, would dominate the collection. Then, at the other end of the spectrum are the uniforms of the armies which have been the enemies of the free world and fought against them in recent decades, such as South Korea, China, North Vietnam; and the homemade rough work uniforms of the Viet Cong.

The field of collecting and displaying complete uniforms is one of the more limited of militaria—especially regarding the space requirements for displaying them.

It should be pointed out that elaborate dress uniforms in themselves are not always sufficient to command interest or value. It is always important to keep in mind the historical association of a particular type of uniform in connection with a specific event or era.

Military headgear also offers a fascinating potential for the collector, and it is in this field that a number of collectors have burgeoned greatly in the last decade. Generally speaking, the modern headgear of military units the world over, since World War II, has still remained in the lower price bracket with only those of the Fascist nations and some of the Communist countries showing any appreciable rise. Justly we might add: helmets and headgear of the United States which were made experimentally, for use only a short time, are also in healthy current demand.

Helmets and headgear offer an excellent potential for the collector as there are so many different types available; both dress and battle from all countries of the world. The mere fact that it is a relatively new field of collecting and a number of good books have recently been written on the subject (with many others on the way) gives the modern collector encouragement, and the feeling that he is part of a field that is catching hold. The most popular items today seem to be the battle-type or steel helmet, rather than the fancy-dress, garrison-type hats with the visors.

There is, of course, limited supply of material as far as the iron curtain nations are concerned. The majority has been brought back as war souvenirs from World War II, the Korean War and the battle going on today in Vietnam. There is no great supply currently on the market, but sufficient pieces seem to be available for collectors now in the field. Helmets of other nations find their way into the market with surprising frequency. At the time they are offered, they are usually in large quantities, having been purchased as surplus from various nations by dealers handling the sales. And, for a time, they seemed to glut the market. It is usually seen, though, that when the supplies dwindle and others do not come to life that these items suddenly start to become much more collectible, and their values rise accordingly. The collector has to have both the courage to buy at the time they are offered, and the perseverance to hold them with the knowledge that eventually they will have value.

MILITARY AND OTHER KNIVES

This is a real hot field of collecting these days. Emphasis is on the small pocket, folding-clasp knives of the post-1900 era, and the military knives of World War I and post-World War II. These two fields were, until recently, the neglected areas of weaponry. Needless to say, the antique-like collecting areas have blossomed in the past twelve to fifteen years to the point where prices have been reaching four figures on certain types. It is only recently that these small pocket clasp knives (many of them give-away advertising items in their day) have truly become collectibles. A few small monographs on the subject have already been written and have sold briskly. It is obvious to anyone in the collecting field that with the publication of a good book on the topic which is bound to come soon, the field will really "boom."

As far as military knives are concerned, there is a great profusion of these from World War II, and in most countries they have been found on the surplus market during the past few years. But, with the diminishing supplies as surplus and the publication of a few good textbooks with identification guides to the various types and models and contract manufacturers, they have been found to have a large following of "buffs," which is constantly growing. They are still relatively easy to acquire at reasonably low prices.

Not to be neglected or "undersold" are the military

bayonets which were more or less ignored until the last two or three years. For many years they were available in huge quantities at both give-away and nominal prices of one to two dollars. Suddenly they came into popularity. Literally, there are hundreds of different types of bayonets. For each of the different types of guns for each country of World War II, there are three or four models of bayonets designed and made; and for each of these models there were various contractors who manufactured them. As you can see, stylistically and marking-wise, the variations are endless. Only recently have many of them been identified; so the field is practically brand-new. There are at least eight or ten good books recently published on bayonet identification. The market activity and fascination in these pieces are exceedingly keen with quite a bright future for the man who is interested.

Of course, as in many other areas of collecting, numerous factors influence the price. It is our opinion that the most important element is the demand; followed by rarity and actual condition of a particular piece.

INSIGNIA AND BUTTONS

There is no disputing anyone, this is a most interesting and diversified field in militaria collecting. There has always been a great number of collectors, but generally speaking prices have been at the level where even the most frugal can afford to build a sizable collection in a comparatively short time.

Although we realize that it is redundant, we must tell you once again that the insignia which seems to have acquired the most interest and reached the highest prices is that of the Axis nations of World War II. It is here, too, where a huge amount of spurious examples crop up; and where the collector must really keep his wits about him, and his knowledge sharpened. The potential for assembling an extremely large collection at a modest monetary investment certainly exists, but it requires foresight and intelligence to acquire a number of pieces which will show a reasonable rate of increased value as time goes on.

The best advice that we can give you, or anyone else can give you, for that matter, is that material from those nations which are the hardest to visit become the most eagerly sought after and consequently the most valuable of collector's items. The collector has his choice of specializing in either cloth or metallic insignia; buttons; or merely helmet insignia. The field is relatively new. Several good books have been written on the subject, primarily on World War II German or Japanese officers' insignia. There are several government bulletins and handbooks which serve as excellent guides to the insignia of various countries. As the demand grows, more new books will be written, and more reprints published.

MEDALS AND DECORATIONS

The very reasons that these were designed and awarded, undoubtedly, account for the fascination with which they are collected and proudly displayed. Most likely a bit of the glamour rubs off on the collector, even though he was not the actual recipient.

This is a big field in collecting, and has followers from all over the world, and in all walks of life. A great many of the medals have possibilities of reaching the upper climes of the value market. The fascination for collecting and ownership is twofold: (1) value of the medal or decoration as a work of art, and its own relative rarity on the collector's scale; (2) historic importance; in many cases it is possible to document the recipient of the medal and the heroic deed for which it was awarded.

Numerous dealers and several good collecting organizations and societies exist in this field. A great amount of material in book form is available with more scheduled for future publication. The scope is wide and each collector has his own opportunity for specializing in a country, a specific war or a period of history. The present-day collector has rather good access to supplies of material through the normal collectors and dealers channels. Current material in many countries is available at moderate prices. A considerable amount of material is still on hand from the early 1900s. Prices indicate merely slight rises within recent years, but judging from experiences in past collectibles, many are most certainly going to "ripen" and mature with the coming years (undoubtedly, enhancing themselves considerably in value). Material of the World War I era especially fits into this category. Only recently some of the more "exotic" of the items has achieved considerable relative value, and every indication points to continued interest and rise in even the more common material of the post-1900 era. A great amount of material since the World War II era is available. With some discrimination and foresight, the collector has the opportunity to put together an interesting and displayable collection. It should not only be educational for himself and his viewers, but it should prove to be a worthy investment as well.

GUNS

Generally speaking, firearms are one of the "hardest" collecting areas. Certainly, since World War II, this field has really "taken off," and achieved almost unbelievable heights (especially in the antique firearms sector).

In present-day collecting of modern weapons, one must play "according to the rules"—the federal government, your state, city, town (and county) have laws pertaining to the ownership of firearms. If this is your field, be sure to apprise yourself of all regulations pertaining to purchase and ownership of such items.

Immediately following the World War II era and until 1968 tremendous quantities of foreign military weapons of all types and from all countries were brought into the United States by importers and sold on the open market to surplus stores and mail-order firms. This material was offered to the public at exceptionally low prices. Such weapons can no longer be imported into this country and among the guns sold there was a very high attrition rate with many converted and altered to sporting material. The remaining, original unaltered military specimens represent interesting potential for future increases in both value and desirability.

Of course, there are many items of post-1900 to World War II era (military weapons) which have always been scarce, but because of their later date had lagged behind price-wise and interest-wise in arms collecting. These are still relatively low-priced on the dealer's market. Although scarce, not always easily available, there is no doubt that their diminishing supply and demand will continue to push their prices up to a point to where they will achieve values on a relative scale with firearms of the nineteenth century.

COMMEMORATIVE GUNS

A most interesting development in the modern sporting guns field is the manufacture of commemorative guns. Many of the largest and most well-known and respected firearms manufacturers have produced, and are currently making, special models of their most famed guns, commemorating specific events and localities. Beginning at a very slow pace in the early 1950s, the manufacturer of such items has hit the market in recent years, and in rather prodigious numbers, creating, in some instances, a rather spectacular collector's market. It might even be said to be almost a matter of which came first, the chicken or the egg? In this case, i.e., was the gun actually created with the collector in mind, or is it now being made with the collector in mind only; or is it made for the event first with the collector following?

Notable examples in this field are: Colt Firearms Company and Winchester Repeating Firearms Company. Probably among the most famed names in the American arms history, these two companies have created especially marked or finished guns for specific events, and made them in very limited quantities. Many of the early issues have risen in price tenfold and twentyfold on the current market. (Of course, this does not mean that everything produced now will increase in proportion.) The market may be very much compared to that of the Jim Beam bottles with the items similar in issuance. Most notables among the Colt issues are its famous Single Action Army Revolver—the identical one issued in 1873 is again in production today. For instance, one of their earliest special issues of this was their "Arizona Territorial Centennial" which was their standard Single Action Army Revolver, but bearing special markings noting the "Arizona Territorial Centennial" on the barrel, with a special serial-number range and a gold finish. Many other issues are similar to this. To date there are over seventy different types of Colt commemorative firearms issued in all models, with the bulk of them being the Single Action Army Revolver. They have standard catalogue values with the early ones being the only ones showing tremendous rises over the issuance prices.

Winchester has generally followed suit, but has not nearly the number of issues to date. A few other gunmakers have entered the market; most notably the Harrington-Richardson Company who has just come out with an exact replica of the famed Officer's Model Springfield breechloading trap-door rifle, issued in limited number, and from all indications not only did it take the market by complete surprise, but also had been completely underestimated as to demand. It appears that items of this sort, if they are well made, and have some history behind them, might very well have a potential in the American arms market—both for current-day collectors and shooters, and will, likewise, possess a very interesting potential for their future increase in price.

Here, too, a word to the wise should suffice that all that glitters is not gold! Following the successful footsteps of Colt, Winchester, Harrington-Richardson, other manufacturers will, undoubtedly, enter the picture, and the market will have a great many other offerings of similar nature. At that point, regardless of the sales pitch and the comparisons of early commemorative prices toward today's prices, the collector should be extremely wary and give considerable thought to what he invests in.

Aim right and we're certain that you will hit the bull's-eye in your successful collecting!

CHAPTER XV

MISCELLANEA

One has but to run down the alphabet from A (Autographs) to Z (Zithers) to see the infinite variety of collectibles around us today. In summary, the following addendum will acquaint you with many other important and worthwhile categories in the area of collecting tomorrow's antiques today.

MODEL SOLDIERS

From ancient days, through the Middle Ages, and right up to the present time, toy soldiers have played a very important part in the life of every boy. Although originally created as playthings, these colorful, precisely made lead and tin military figures are of such historical significance that they have earned recognition in many private collections and museums around the world. Historians, artists, costume designers and military men find them invaluable in their work and studies. It has been recorded that great leaders such as Eisenhower and Churchill considered them instructive, and that Napoleon moved his model military army around like chessmen in planning war strategy, as well as his own coronation.

Military models were first made of wood, ceramics, brass and glass; and even in precious silver for young princes and sons of the nobility. There is historical reference, but exactly how well substantiated we are not certain, that lead soldiers, *soldats de plomb*, were first made in France and by no less a personage then Louis XIII when he was dauphin.

The earliest commercial toy soldiers in pure tin, called *Zinnsoldat*, were manufactured in Germany in the eighteenth century by the tinsmith family of Hilpert. Tin models continued to be made until the material became too costly for the huge scale of mass production; and then lead was welded to molten tin. The figures were flats; two-dimensional pieces pressed together with the alloys poured between. They were crude, especially in comparison to the ones later to be manufactured in France in solid lead. During this period Germany controlled the toy market and soon followed suit with the three-dimensional solids. England entered the industry in the late nineteenth century and quickly captured the retail market which it dominates today. The collecting of model soldiers has become such an important hobby that they are now manufactured in the United States, Sweden, Italy, Holland and many other countries. There are collector's clubs and publications; and many magazine articles have been written on the subject. Among several excellent books we highly recommend: *Model Soldiers—A Collec-*

tor's Guide by John G. Garratt (Seeley Service & Co., London). This is a comprehensive and definitive work and has an extensive list of collector's societies and world-wide museums exhibiting model soldiers.

In recent years the hobby of painting and assembling model soldiers has become most popular. Good kits are available in hobby shops and a large supply source is Polk's Hobbies (New York) which also issues a Collector Soldier catalogue. *The Model Soldier Manual . . . A Basic Guide* by Peter J. Blum (illustrations by Clyde A. Risley who with William F. Imrie is a leading expert on military miniatures—their firm is known as I/R Miniatures) is an easy-to-understand "how to do it" book.

Model soldiers have, during the past ten years, made an advance into plastics. Leads, happily, are still being manufactured, and undoubtedly always will be. However, plastics are not to be disregarded, whether you like them or don't. No matter what you are assembling, no collection is thorough or complete without following chronological sequence. Take our word for it, there will be a terrific generation gap in collecting model soldiers if plastics are not included. With the rapid advancements in science and the discoveries from outer space, it is reasonably safe to assume that all the precious metals and man-made substances in use today may within a comparatively short span of time become relics of the past.

MINIATURES

We like to look upon these little scale models as the "world of inanimate Lilliputians." Especially today when many of us live in smaller houses or apartments; and others move frequently from place to place, collecting in this field has come into great popularity and favor. There are miniatures in practically everything: dolls, dollhouses; home furnishings in china, glass and silver; toys, automobiles, toy soldiers, bottles, musical instruments, ships, locomotives and railroad cars, aircraft, buildings, photographs and pictures, playing cards, books, animals, birds, fish; and complete villages, towns and cities with tiny people as real as Gulliver's own "Lilliputians."

Each month *Hobbies* magazine features "Miniaturia," a department conducted by the Reverend Stuart A. Parvin. In this publication, you will also find advertising columns under the heading "Miniatures for Sale" which seems to us an easy and quick way to get started in this field. Books on the subject include: *Dolls and Miniatures with Their Prices at Auction* by Hopkinson; *Antique Miniature Furniture in Great Britain and America* by Jane Toller; *The Dollhouse Book* by Estelle Worrell; *Miniature Lamps* by Frank and Ruth Smith. For titles of books in the group of miniatures in which you are most interested, consult your local librarian. You will find interesting miniatures in shops everywhere. The most unique collections we have seen are the highly specialized ones. We met a man who has over five hundred miniature bottles of well-known liquor brands. It was dramatically displayed in a glass cabinet behind his bar. "A most inexpensive collection," he told us, "as I gathered them on trains, planes and ships. In fact, porters, stewards and hostesses gladly gave them to me, and almost tipped me for taking them away and relieving them of the disposal nuisance and responsibility." Unfortunately, we can't think of any other collectibles as simple and inexpensive to acquire.

NAPKIN RINGS

Almost as quaint as the old-fashioned buttonhook, napkin rings may need some explaining to our young readers. Before the innovation of paper napkins, napkin rings were used in practically every home. Usually of silver and nicely decorated or personally monogrammed for each member of the family, they added an intimate note to the dining table. In well-run homes fresh linen napkins were distributed each day for use at dinner and breakfast the next morning. In less meticulous families they often served several days and literally were not a pleasant sight. Napkin rings have returned to the shops and homes today and we do not know whether it is the revival of an old custom, or the promotional activities of devout ecologists and conservationists as an aid to the problems of waste disposal. The old ones sell for fair prices in antique shops and are popular collectibles; and the new ones should also have a good future.

EPHEMERA

Anything of a very short life (*Funk & Wagnalls*).

This is the expert collector's eight-letter word for every type of printed matter of a temporary nature—advertising, Christmas cards, valentines, posters, picture postcards, etc.

When Johann Gutenberg invented the printing machine in the fifteenth century, he had little realization that his brain child would be such a great contribution to the world of art. Magnificent printed material comes to us every day and, to the beginning collector in this field, decisions on what to assemble may appear baffling. Specialization is the fast-and-true rule in this classification. Select the category which appeals to you and concentrate on that and that alone. For instance:

Christmas Cards: Probably the first commercially published Christmas cards in the United States were around the mid-1800s. Back in those days the average person did not receive much mail, and these early greeting cards were so novel that they were cherished and kept in albums. During the sentimental Victorian period, collecting began in earnest. Examining early specimens we find these cards were uninteresting in graphic design and except for the most costly ones, produced on inexpensive paper. It was their sentiments and scarcity which built up the collector's interest. Perhaps, it was not until the 1950s that Christmas cards really began to take on new, exciting creativity. Despite the fact that production is overwhelmingly great, not many people save them. This, in itself, offers a wide avenue for new collectors. The cards of today are truly magnificent works of art, and it's a scandalous shame to see them thrown away.

Greeting Cards: Name the occasion and you will find a made-to-order card—Mother's Day, Father's Day, Easter, Passover, birthdays, anniversaries, Thanksgiving, St. Patrick's Day, confirmation, Bar Mitzvah, graduation, sympathy, humorous, retirement, travel, friendship. They're clever, imaginative and colossal!

Valentines: These old sweethearts of cards have long

been big items of collecting. Valentines came into existence centuries ago and developed from the beautiful handwritten letters in poetry and prose which sweethearts exchanged on the romantic festival of St. Valentine (February 14). The Victorians loved them, but in the early twentieth century valentines took on a comic tone and, as they justly deserved, faded into oblivion. Around twenty years ago card manufacturers revived the valentine, and once again they are flourishing. Probably, though, they will never come into the collecting prominence they enjoyed years ago. Something seems to be missing; perhaps it is the lace and frills or that Cupid isn't our hero any longer. We have discussed this with our friend, Mrs. Dorothy Schling, Director of the Scott-Fanton Museum (Danbury, Connecticut). She is an expert in this field and has a prized collection of old valentines. In her opinion the valentine is a worthy collectible; collectors of current valentines are few which makes the field uncompetitive; and unless collecting is pursued, the annals of the valentine will lose the important chronological sequence of this particular period. Two good books on the subject are: *History of Valentines,* by Ruth W. Lee; *Valentine and Its Origins* by Frank Staff.

Advertising: A wide, tall and handsome subject. Here is where one meets the rivalry in the graphic arts. Artists, designers, writers and printers deserve great praise for the spectacular production of folders, brochures, catalogues, annual reports, signs and posters, which are all outstanding examples of art. Never has there been a better selection for the collector, but there again selectivity of subject is of the utmost importance.

In this field of printed ephemera are menus, match covers, letterheads, business cards and calendars. We know a man who specializes in steamship menus which he began quite a few years ago. The United States Line, French Line, Cunard Line and all the others are represented in his fascinating collection. Now, that travel by ship is fast sailing into the lost horizon, a collection of this nature is not only unique, but should have vast importance and value as time goes on. Many men and women collect match covers. These are colorful and interesting. Calendars are good collectibles, but not quite in the immediate ephemeral group as they are usually for an entire year. However, a real collector's item, if you can obtain one, is: *The Needham & Grohmann 30-Year Calendar to Complete the Twentieth Century 1971–2000.* Privately published by this New York advertising agency to commemorate its fortieth anniversary, this is a handsomely designed and printed book, attractively bound in a hard cover. In calendar collecting, 1971 was an auspicious year with the advent of the National Monday Holiday Plan which made the following date changes: Washington's Birthday (third Monday in February); Memorial Day (last Monday in May); Columbus Day (second Monday in October); and Veterans' Day (fourth Monday in October). Corporate material of this nature is definitely "collectible."

The list in this category is limitless and includes premium inserts, wrappers, labels and tags. Advertisements, per se are most important especially if you build up a collection in a specific field: automobiles, hotels and motels, food items, airlines, fashions, etc. Or, concentrate on an era—1940s, 1950s, 1960s, 1970s. A collection that shows serious study and has extensive coverage will eventually show the greatest possible potential in value.

Posters: As we know them today, posters came into existence in Europe in the early nineteenth century when devotees of the arts began to assemble theatrical and opera posters for their documentary interest. It was in the mid-1800s when the "poster craze," as this form of collecting was often called, reached America. It began when leading publishers followed the European custom of announcing new books and magazines through the advertising medium of small posters and window signs. At first they were in black and white with limited printed text and no illustrations. Later they were produced in color lithography and signed by the publishers' own illustrators. The demand for these posters was tremendous and often surpassed publication sales. Advertisers then became shrewd enough to avail themselves of the powerful sales power of the artistic poster. The poster fever was highly contagious, and socially it became the fashion to give "poster parties" in which people dressed up as poster figures. Then, the fad subsided, but it left a deep impression on American advertising art.

The "poster craze" has returned with more vigor, enthusiasm and excitement. And, there is a greater variety of interesting and worthwhile material for the collector. Book stores and art shops are flooded with reprints of old posters by Toulouse-Lautrec, Miró, Matisse and other famous artists from $1.00 up. These are fine for decorative pieces in homes and offices, but not the collectibles.

Many poster collectors have been fortunate enough to come upon the great posters of World War I when there was no radio or television, and this medium offered the most forceful manner of mass communication. Leading artists such as James Montgomery Flagg, J. C. Leyendecker, Joseph Pennell, Ben Shahn and others contributed their talents to recruiting, national defense and other patriotic posters. Good posters of this type sell from $5.00 up to several hundreds. World War II posters are in great demand and particularly the works signed by James Montgomery Flagg, Ben Shahn, John Atherton, Joseph Binder, Symeon Shimm, E. McKnight Kauffer and Norman Rockwell.

As a beginner in collecting posters, concentration should be on subject and artist. The categories are many: opera, movies, personalities, theatre, concerts, circus, political, travel, product advertising, causes (Red Cross, Boy Scouts, etc.). Institutional posters of important industrial firms are an excellent source, such as General Dynamics "Peaceful Uses of the Atom" by Erik Nitsche.

Begin to read about posters. Excellent references are: *The American Poster* by Edgar Breitenbach and Margaret Cogswell; *American Poster* by Jack Amon; *Pictorial History of the American Circus* by John and Alice Durant; *The Poster: Its History and Its Art* by Ervine Metzl. Your librarian will help you with other titles. Poster exhibits are often on display in leading museums such as the Metropolitan Museum of Art and the Museum of Modern Art. Many museums have art bulletins in which you will find good material on posters.

Subways, buses and railroad stations are excellent

places to see the latest posters. In lobbies of theatres, con-
cert halls and opera houses you will come across great
personality posters. If you have a friend in printing or
advertising, solicit his interest in your field of collecting,
and you'll probably be able to obtain exciting posters
right off the presses. And, by all means watch the high-
way billboard advertising. These are called 24-sheet
posters, and although you won't be collecting these gi-
ants, you will most likely find adaptations of the same
messages in regular poster size. Choose your subject and
make your own public announcement of what you are
collecting to every one you know. You'll find people more
than willing to aid you and before long you'll have
posters enough to paper a room in your home.

PICTURE POSTCARDS

These are the "Having a wonderful time, wish you were
here" greetings. Souvenir cards came into existence in the
mid-1800s. In those days they were novel, showing views
of cities, towns, inns, hotels, and cost but a few pennies
or were given away gratuitously (postage was one cent).
Recipients placed them in an album; and if they had not
done so we would have fewer historical records of how
people, landscapes and buildings looked in the past. Since
the development of Kodachrome, picture postcards are
magnificent specimens of art and photography and desirable collectibles. A good assemblage would be to collect
them in categories: national parks, historic shrines, land
and sea scenes, mountain views, hotels and inns—any
category which appeals to you. The scope is wider than
ever with the increase in international travel.

CLOCKS AND WATCHES

Time never stands still in this field of collecting. *Hobbies* has a monthly feature, "On Time," conducted by Orville R. Hagans, which takes readers into the collecting of antique clocks. It is advisable to become acquainted with antique clocks and watches, and then you will be armed to carry on with all the wonderful timepieces of today which, in their own right, will naturally become the "antiques" of tomorrow. This is a very important field and we do encourage you to get started by (1) writing to the National Association of Watch and Clock Collectors (Columbia, Pennsylvania); (2) reading a few good books on the subject: *American Clocks and Clock Makers* by Carl W. Drepperd, *The Collector's Dictionary of Clocks* by Alan Lloyd, *Watches* by Cecil Clutton. The list is endless and your librarian will help you to select the books most important to you; (3) become acquainted with the outstanding clock and watchmakers: Longines, Omega, Rolex, Tourneau, Hamilton, Seth Thomas, Waltham, Bulova, Westclox—these are merely a few well-known names.

Look through the magazines, browse in the stores and you will quickly decide for yourself which timepieces have "a future." Among the ones we like are: the world clock which tells you at a glance the time anywhere in the world from Albany to Zurich. It has a fully transistorized battery movement and sells for approximately $130. Bulova's Accutron watch is a late twentieth-century instrument. Less than $200. The Rolex in its indestructible Oyster case reflects today's precision. Around

$255. There is a Pedometer for less than $10; electric alarm clocks with radio that show the date and day of week.

Character and "comic" watches are a big field. Prices are high for the old ones as there are so few in existence. If you had any of these as a kid you might like to know that a 1934 Ingersoll Big Bad Wolf wrist watch is listed on the dealer's market around $200; a 1934 Ingersoll Popeye pocket watch at $350; New Haven Orphan Annie wrist watch $75. Other watches in the $100 group are: Lone Ranger, Mickey Mouse, Roy Rogers, Howdy Doody, Babe Ruth, Dizzy Dean, Superman, Pepsi-Cola, and Captain Marvel. Among the caricature watches on the market today are W. C. Fields, Laurel and Hardy and the Democrat and Republican watches. Each of these will, undoubtedly, become collector's items.

HANDICRAFTS

It is encouraging to observe today's handicraft activities throughout the world; and the manner in which skilled and talented craftsmen are earnestly contributing to art and aesthetic culture.

Mass production which plays a very important part in our mode of living has brought not only great comforts, but also the advantages of more time and leisure for pursuing an art, craft or hobby.

The handicrafts of today are fine examples of workmanship and equal in design and beauty to those of the past, and, too, faithfully reflect the progress of our era. Our native crafts began with the American Indian and developed with the colonists who brought glass blowing, woodworking, metalsmithing, scrimshaw, knitting, lacemaking, embroidery, spinning and weaving, candlemaking and all the other arts to these shores. Collecting today in this field is wide and varied and the categories include: pottery, handmade rugs and carpets, wooden articles, needlework, puppets and marionettes, silversmithing, enameling, bookbinding, basketry, stenciling, block printing, serigraphy (silk-screening), illuminating, lettering and calligraphy. The old crafts have survived and many new ones have been added. *Yankee* magazine is an excellent monthly publication for becoming acquainted with the crafts of today.

RECORDINGS

We, of the twentieth century, are the music makers. Whether it is good, bad, indifferent and will survive is difficult to determine. Records are very important collectibles, but it is most important to be discerning as there is so much music around us today. Collectors of old records can play it on the cool side as their entire choice is infinitesimal compared to the gigantic volumes of recordings being issued today.

The old 78s were not produced in quantity and were easily broken; thus not many of collector's importance are in existence. Today's records are practically unbreakable and produced in the volume of thousands and thousands.

The music of this era depicts our way of life and has a vital audio message. If you wish to refer to it as Modern Pop—it began with the rock and roll in the mid-1950s, then danced into the western jogs, folk music, soul music and everything else we call it. The Beatles were the initiators; now off the scene, but most likely of all will go down in the annals of this age of music. We, ourselves, don't dig too much "mod" as becoming tomorrow's antiques. Much of it deserves to be preserved, but we are fearful of the mass production and the indestructibility of the records themselves. Too many will be on future markets and this includes opera records and Broadway shows.

Voice recordings, a poet reciting his works, an author reading his stories, an actor delivering his lines, are collectibles, provided the people are accepted and popular at the time. From our own collectibles we cite: Dylan Thomas reciting *A Child's Christmas in Wales*, Somerset Maugham reading from "The Three Fat Women of Antibes," John Barrymore in Shakespearian roles and T. S. Eliot reading his own poetry. These, we know, are prized collectibles. There are recordings of John F. Kennedy, Franklin Roosevelt and other Presidents of the United States. The first President who has been mentioned as recording is Benjamin Harrison in office 1889–93. Collecting the recordings of Presidents cannot fail in potential worth.

Collect in a discriminate manner and you will certainly do well.

BOOKS

Bibliophiles (those who love books) are not for the most part collectors in our usage of the word. They are, however, collectors in the avid manner in which they purchase books to read, enjoy and add to their own personal libraries. Many of them, we suspect, would be amazed at the value of their books, if they had any sound knowledge of the collecting field. Once in discussing the "detective story" with a learned friend of ours, he told us, as though we had never heard it before, that Edgar Allan Poe was the inventor of the modern detective story. His astonishment came when we mentioned, rather casually, that *The Murders in the Rue Morgue* (1843) jumped from $.12½ on publication to $25,000 in 1926. The last we heard is that a volume of this book is in the rare book collection of the New York Public Library.

The best introduction we can give you on collecting books are the two volumes by Van Allen Bradley: *Gold in Your Attic* and *More Gold in Your Attic*. We have consulted publishers, booksellers and book buyers, hoping to obtain concrete opinions of which books today will be the collector's items of tomorrow. They were all hesitant in expressing their views, and the best clues we can pass along to you are from autograph experts. Big prices are being paid today for the manuscripts of Tennessee Williams, Norman Mailer, Ernest Hemingway, T. S. Eliot, Georges Simenon, Carl Sandburg. Therefore, isn't it reasonable to assume that books by these authors will appreciate in valuation?

JEWELRY

Rings, pins, earrings, cuff links, bracelets, tie tabs and charms—jewelry is an interesting collectible. Here, we think is a great opportunity for creative collecting; along the lines of a collection of rings with the emblems of men's colleges; or twenty-five year service pins from various large corporations. Merely suggestions.

COMIC BOOKS

There are avid collectors of comic books and magazines. These include tales of laughter, science fiction, fantasy, mystery, movies and imagination in every form. The old comic books have real value and usually Volume I, Number 1 is the most valuable. A cursory glance of a 1971 price list shows how the collecting crowd has made the prices skyrocket:

Captain America, No. 1	$175.00
Marvel Mysteries, Nos. 13–26	25.00–38.00
Super Dooper, No. 26	20.00
Captain Marvel, No. 36	15.00
Batman, No. 2	50.00
Batman, Nos. 7–11	25.00

It appears to be a good idea to find out what the kids are reading, and tell them to keep the peanut butter and jelly off the pages as there may be gold mixed with the printer's ink.

Collecting can take one anywhere—into the world of pop art, bells, ship and railroad models, mobiles, boxes, decoys, sheet music, Christmas tree ornaments, furniture, musical instruments, wood carvings, newspapers, magazines and automobiles.

Keep your eyes wide open for everything that is new today as it will be an "antique of tomorrow." Your fun is just beginning! Remember there will always be something "new under the moon" to collect—and perhaps soon, from the moon itself!

CHAPTER XVI

CAVEAT EMPTOR

Practically every writer on antiques feels compelled to issue a "Buyer Beware" warning on fakes and reproductions. In collecting the antiques of tomorrow, actually there should be no immediate concern with problems of this nature. At least, not until the demand becomes greater than the supply or when prices reach values which make camouflage appear profitable to the unscrupulous.

However, we do feel that it is never too early to be alerted to spurious and imitative pieces. Cunning replicas of originals by established and successful manufacturers could, almost, at any time become the target for copycats plotting a way to make quick money. Imitators, as such, might be too clever to risk "illegal falsity," but smart enough to stay within the law by manufacturing items so deceptive in appearance that, to the guillible, they would pass for what they are not. Then, of course, there are the completely illegal forgers. Naturally, this is all our own supposition, but to be forewarned is to be fore-armed.

As protection against the possibility of such an un-pleasant occurrence, here are a few simple rules, known by all expert collectors of true antiques:

(1) *KNOWLEDGE OF YOUR SUBJECT*

For easy illustrative purposes, let us take paperweights as a hypothetical case. You admire them and would like to be a collector, but know little or nothing about the subject. The first rudiments are to read everything you can find about paperweights in books and magazines. Your local library will be helpful, and if you do not find what you want in the Index under "Paperweights," your librarian will refer you to the huge volume entitled *Subject Guide to Books in Print* (the Publisher's Trade List Annual).

Extremely important—visit museums and see the ex-hibits of rare paperweights. This will give you an im-mediate appreciation of their beauty and variety. Try to locate a collector's club and join. This is also an ex-cellent way to see what others are collecting, and an op-portunity to obtain friendly advice. Under each chapter we have attempted to give you names of clubs devoted to the various categories. (See Appendix.)

Serious study of this nature may seem to you a tortuous assignment, but you will soon find it absorbing fun. It will pay off and you will acquire the same knowledge as other experts in the field. Starting off in a superficial manner usually proves disastrous as you will make wrong purchases and spend your money unwisely.

(2) *KNOWLEDGE OF THE MARKET*

This is threefold—the manufacturers, the dealers and the collectors (you).

MANUFACTURERS: Familiarity with the reputation of the various producers is most essential, as it is important to know the recognized manufacturers or the individual artisans whose work is directly distributed through dealers. Become acquainted with the hallmarks or other features of identification and you are less likely to be fooled on true authenticity. *Sensory perception* often helps to determine the real from the false. This is something you do develop as you acquire expertise, and literally regret not knowing when you make a bad purchase or two and realize your errors! Therefore, cultivate the practice of examining pieces carefully. Experienced dealers and curators of museums can almost tell intuitively the genuineness of an object by how it looks and how it feels.

Keep vigilant on Limited Editions. When a reputable manufacturer announces the number of an item to be issued and the molds to be destroyed, it is a hard-and-fast rule that no more will appear on the market.

Here is a general guide to watch out for to avoid bad buys. Overruns of a promised issue by firms of an unstable reputation. A company encountering financial difficulties and attempting not to go bankrupt by flooding the market with inferior items from a still-existing master mold. Downright deceptiveness of fake and forgery.

DEALERS: It is most likely that a majority of your purchases will be made from dealers. The franchised dealer, therefore, is important to you and has the same reputation to maintain as the manufacturer. The big names in china, glass, silver and other classifications are most choosy in assigning distributorships. A few words of admonition are: when purchasing pieces of collectible importance have caution where you buy, especially in strange cities and when you are in a hurry. Watch out on vacations that you don't fall into tourist's traps and think that you are getting a bargain when you are buying a fake.

COLLECTORS: This is YOU and every other collector. We have included you in everything said; not to alarm you but to set you off as an expert in your chosen field. Again we stress, a reputable dealer is your best friend. This is even more true in used articles than in the factory new. However, as you attain knowledge and confidence in your judgment, you can then pit your wits against any one.

Now we come to *prices* which are deserving of discussion. When you purchase a piece (current) by a manufacturer, the price is definitely established on the retail market. You are on safe ground here, but once an item is no longer available in shops and stores, it becomes the possession of a private collector or enters the dealer's market. Trading then begins, exactly as on the stock market, with a buying price and a selling price (an approximate increase of 35–50 per cent). Demand is probably the most significant factor with scarcity and rarity close seconds, and condition is a determinant. You can keep posted on current prices from various Price Guides, or through the *Antique Trader Weekly,* and other collecting publications in which the field has many. As you well know by now, the word "antique" is ambiguous; *scarcity, rarity* and *historical* significance often superseding actual age as collectibles.

If you stay with your chosen field and follow the trends by diligent reading and discussion with fellow collectors, you will quickly learn the market, what to buy, when to sell and how to do it. You will also quickly learn that an advertised or a catalogue listed price is not always the one that you can receive for your own piece . . . and, in some cases, even though an item has an established catalogue price there are just no takers at any price! It is also essential to know that regardless of an established catalogue or dealer's retail price, it certainly is very difficult for you, as a private individual, to get that price or even a close proximity to it. After all, the dealer, or the person advertising his wares has to have an edge to make it profitable for him to do so. Depending on the demand for the piece you are selling (and, of course, its relative rarity and condition) you will most likely realize anywhere from 20 per cent to 50 per cent less than the top advertised retail value, if sold to dealers or at a collector's market. You do have, however, a number of outlets available that will give you the opportunity to achieve the full and top retail value for that item. It is just these outlets and possibilities that make the field of collecting such an interesting one in the value department! All it takes on your part is a little extra effort and patience.

Like anything else, if you are in a hurry you can never realize the full potential from your efforts. As previously

70. Mechanical Banks,
Private Collection of
F. H. Griffith.

71. "Mary Poppins" Doll
by Peggy Nesbit,
courtesy Tudor House.

72. Madame Alexander Portrait Dolls, Alexander Doll Company, Inc.

73. Madame Alexander
"Pussy Cat" Doll,
Alexander Doll Company, Inc.

74. "Little Women" Dolls,
Alexander Doll
Company, Inc.

75. "Children, Hope of
the World" (first American
art medal made from
hammered metal),
by sculptor Nina Winkel,
photo courtesy Medallic
Art Company.

76. Apollo 11 Medal by sculptor Boris Buzan, courtesy Medallic Art Company.

77. Apollo 14 Medal by sculptor Ralph J. Menconi, courtesy Medallic Art Company.

78. Richard Nixon Medal, courtesy Medallic Art Company.

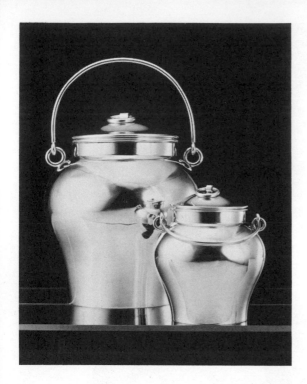

79. Tiffany Silver Covered Urns Copied from Eighteenth-century Danish Midwives' Lunch Pails.

80. Tiffany Silver Egg Basket.

81. Tiffany Silver Rabbit Paperweights.

82. Boxes by Tiffany.

83. NASA Cards, by United States
Playing Card Company.

84. Lead-crystal Annual Mug
by Kosta, courtesy Georg Jensen, Inc.

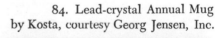

85. Kosta's "The Family,"
Mother, 1970, Father, 1971,
courtesy Georg Jensen, Inc.

86. Orrefors Crystal,
courtesy Fisher Bruce
& Co.

87. Orrefors Crystal,
courtesy Fisher Bruce & Co.

88. Owl by Steuben Glass.

89. Eagle by Steuben Glass.

90. "Love" by Steuben Glass.

91. Crystal Paperweight
with Interior Threads of
White Glass
by Steuben Glass.

92. 1971 Crystal Coin Plate, by Imperial
Glass Corporation.

93. 1970 Christmas Plate, by Imperial Glass Corporation.

mentioned, the numerous collectors journals and periodicals have classified advertising columns in which thousands of collectors the country over run advertisements for both buying and selling. The cost of an advertisement is most nominal in almost every one of these journals. All that is necessary is to write an attractively worded ad, place it and then be patient for a month or so in the hope that when the ad appears you can make a suitable marriage between your item for sale and a collector somewhere else in the United States looking for that particular piece. Of course, it is not all "roses." It does require a bit more effort; for instance, sometimes a certain amount of cross-correspondence is necessary between buyer and seller. You must be able to pack and ship the item and, of course, you must guarantee its authenticity and be able to take it back for full refund if the buyer is not satisfied. These are all part and parcel of doing business through the mail. Undoubtedly, a large percentage of dealers in business today started those very same businesses as collectors who dabbled part-time in mail order and found the field fruitful enough to enter full-time.

In summary: We hope that we have given you some sound advice. Definitely, we can promise you fun, excitement and a personal pride of assembling today the antiques of tomorrow. In the vernacular of "Peanuts"— "What do you think our chances are of winning today?"

Good, we'd say!

APPENDIX

RECOMMENDED READING

Prodigious research has gone into the preparation of this book. In addition to reading voluminous works on each specific subject, we have studied encyclopedias, manufacturers' catalogues and brochures. The best advice we can offer, in order to keep you up-to-date in your area of collecting, is that you consult regularly with your book dealer or local library.

AUTOGRAPHS

Benjamin, Mary A., *Autographs: A Key to Collecting*. 1946. (reissued 1963) Walter R. Benjamin Autographs, Inc., 790 Madison Ave., New York, N.Y. 10021

Hamilton, Charles, *Collecting Autographs and Manuscripts*. 1961. University of Oklahoma Press, Norman, Oklahoma 73069

——, *Scribblers & Scoundrels*. 1968. Paul S. Eriksson, Inc., 119 W. 57, New York, N.Y. 10019

Notlep, Robert, *The Autograph Collector; A New Guide.* 1969. Crown Publishers, 419 Park Ave. S., New York, N.Y. 10016

BANKS

Griffith, F. H., *New Illustrated Mechanical Bank Booklet.* 1972. F. H. Griffith, P. O. Box 10644, Pittsburgh, Pa. 15235
Whiting, Hubert B., *Old Iron Still Banks.* 1965. Forward's Color Productions, Inc., Manchester, Vermont.

BOTTLES

Hastin, Bud, *Bud Hastin's Avon Bottle Encyclopedia.* Bud Hastin, Box 4868, Kansas City, Missouri 64134
Munsey, Cecil, *The Illustrated Guide to Collecting Bottles.* Hawthorn Books, Inc., 70 Fifth Ave., New York, N.Y. 10011
Stuart, Lynn R., *Stuart's Book on Avon Bottles.* Lynn R. Stuart, P. O. Box 862, Gilbert, Arizona 85234
Western Collector, *Western Collector's Handbook and Price Guide to Avon Collectables.* 1970. Western Collector, 511 Harrison St., San Francisco, California 94105
——, *Western Collector's Handbook and Price Guide to EZRA BROOKS Ceramic Decanters.* 1970. Western World Publishers.
Yount, John, *Bottle Collector's Handbook and Price Guide.* 1969. Educator Books, 10 N. Main St., Drawer 32, San Angelo, Texas 76901

BUTTONS

Brown, Dorothy Foster, *Button Parade.* 1969. Mid-America Book Company, Main St., Leon, Iowa 50144
Johnson, David F., *Military Buttons and Uniforms.* Century House, Watkins Glen, N.Y. 14891
Luscomb, Sally, *The Collector's Encyclopedia of Buttons.* 1967. Crown Publishers, 419 Park Ave. S., New York, N.Y. 10016
Roberts, Catherine, *Who's Got the Button?* 1962. David McKay Co., 750 Third Avenue, New York, N.Y. 10017

CLOCKS AND WATCHES

Cumhaill, P. W., *Investing in Clocks and Watches.* 1967. Clarkson N. Potter, Inc., 419 Park Avenue S., New York, N.Y. 10016
Palmer, Brooks, *The Book of American Clocks.* 1950. The Macmillan Company, 866 Third Ave., New York, N.Y. 10022

DOLLS AND TOYS

Coleman, Dorothy, Elizabeth, and Evelyn, *Collector's Encyclopedia of Dolls*. 1969. Crown Publishers, 419 Park Ave. S., New York, N.Y. 10016

Dicicco, Laurel M., *Doll Collectors' Treasures*. Laurel M. Dicicco, 14916 Cholame, Victoryville, California 92392

Fraser, Antonia, *A History of Toys*. 1966. Delacorte Press, 750 Third Ave., New York, N.Y. 10017

Hertz, Louis, *The Toy Collector*. Funk & Wagnalls, 380 Madison Ave., New York, N.Y. 10017

Hillier, Mary, *Pageant of Toys*. 1965. Taplinger Publishing Company, 29 E. Tenth St., New York, N.Y. 10003

White, Gwen, *Dolls of the World*. 1963. Charles T. Branford Co., 28 Union St., Newton Centre, Mass. 02159

FIREARMS AND MILITARIA

Atwood, James P. (Major), *Daggers and Edged Weapons of Hitler's Germany*. 1965. Privately Printed.

Chapel, Charles Edward, *Complete Book of Gun Collecting*. 1960. Coward-McCann, 200 Madison Avenue, New York, N.Y. 10016

Guidice, Elio and Del, *Italian Military Uniforms, 1934–1968*. Bramante (Italian)

Hicks, James R. (Major), *U.S. Military Firearms 1776–1956*. Privately printed.

Kannik, Preben, *Military Uniforms of the World in Color*. 1968. The Macmillan Company, 866 Third Ave., New York, N.Y. 10022

Latham, John, *British Military Swords from 1800 to the Present Day*. 1966. Crown Publishers, 419 Park Ave. S., New York, N.Y. 10016

Madis, George, *The Winchester Book*. 1961. 607 N. Windomere Ave., Dallas, Texas 75208

Peterson, Harold L., *A History of Knives*. 1966. Charles Scribner's Sons, 597 Fifth Ave., New York, N.Y. 10017

———, *American Knives*. 1958. Charles Scribner's Sons.

———, *Remington Historical Treasure of American Guns*, 1966. The Benjamin Company, 485 Madison Ave., New York, N.Y. 10022

Rankin, Robert H. (Col.), *Uniforms of the Army*. 1968. G. P. Putnam's Sons, 200 Madison Avenue, New York, N.Y. 10016

Serven, James E., *Colt Firearms*. 1954. Foundation Press, 170 Old Country Road, Mineola, N.Y. 11501

——, *The Collecting of Guns.* 1964. Bonanza Books, 419 Park Avenue S., New York, N.Y. 10016

Wilson, R. L., *Colt Commemorative Firearms.* 1969. Kidwell.

NOTE: All "Firearms and Militaria" books listed may be ordered from N. Flayderman & Co., Inc., New Milford, Conn. 06776

GLASS

Eberle, Irmengarde, *The New World of Glass.* 1963. Dodd, Mead, & Co., 79 Madison Ave., New York, N.Y. 10016

Plaut, James, *Steuben Glass.* 1951. Bittner.

Stcuben Glass, *Engraved Crystal.* Privately printed by Steuben Glass, Fifth Ave. & 56th St., New York, N.Y. 10022

——, *Selection of Engraved Crystal.* 1961. Privately printed by Steuben Glass.

——, *Poetry in Crystal.* 1963. Privately printed by Steuben Glass.

MODEL SOLDIERS

Arnold, Arnold, *Book of Toy Soldiers.* 1965. Random House, 201 E. 50th St., New York, N.Y. 10022

Harris, Henry, *Model Soldiers.* 1962. G. P. Putnam's Sons, 200 Madison Avenue, New York, N.Y. 10022

——, *Collecting Model Soldiers.* 1971. Abelard-Schuman, Ltd., 257 Park Ave. S., New York, N.Y. 10010

MUSIC BOXES

Mosoriak, Roy, *The Curious History of Music Boxes.* 1943. Lightner. May be ordered from *Hobbies* magazine, 1006 S. Michigan Ave., Chicago, Ill. 60605

PAPERWEIGHTS

Cloak, Evelyn Campbell, *Glass Paperweights of the Bergstrom Collection.* 1969. Crown Publishers, 419 Park Ave. S., New York, N.Y. 10016

Elville, E. M., *Paperweights and Other Glass Curiosities.* 1967. Spring Books (London).

Hollister, Paul, *The Encyclopedia of Glass Paperweights.* 1968. Clarkson N. Potter, 419 Park Ave. S., New York, N.Y. 10016

Jokelson, Paul, *Sulphides: The Art of Cameo Incrustation*. 1968. Thomas Nelson Inc., Copewood & Davis Sts., Camden, N.J. 08103

Melvin, Jean, *American Glass Paperweights and Their Makers*. 1967. Thomas Nelson Inc.

PLAYING CARDS

Hargrave, Catherine, *A History of Playing Cards*. 1931. Dover Publications, 180 Varick St., New York, N.Y. 10014

Tilley, Roger, *Playing Cards*. 1967. G. P. Putnam's Sons, 200 Madison Avenue, New York, N.Y. 10016

PORCELAIN AND POTTERY

Boncz, Clara, *Herend China*. 1966. Branden Press, 221 Columbus Ave., Boston, Mass. 02116

Cox, Warren, *The Book of Pottery and Porcelain*. 1970. 419 Park Ave. S., New York, N.Y. 10016

Ketchum, W. C., Jr., *The Pottery and Porcelain Collectors' Handbook*. Funk & Wagnalls Inc., 201 Park Ave., New York, N.Y. 10003

Owen, Pat, *The Story of Bing & Grøndahl Christmas Plates*. 1962. Viking Import House, Burnham Lane, Dayton, Ohio.

——, *The Story of Royal Copenhagen Christmas Plates*. 1962. Viking Import House.

Platt, Dorothy Pickard, *The Story of Pickard China*. 1971. Privately printed.

Trimble, Alberta C., *Modern Porcelain; Today's Treasures, Tomorrow's Traditions*. 1962. Bonanza Books, 419 Park Ave. S., New York, N.Y. 10016

Wykes-Joyce, Max, *7000 Years of Pottery and Porcelain*. 1958. Dufour Editions Inc., Chester Springs, Pa. 19425

SPOONS

Hardt, Anton, *Souvenir Spoons of the 90's*. 1962. Hardt, 335 Bleecker St., New York, N.Y. 10014

——, *Adventuring Further in Souvenir Spoons*. 1966. Hardt.

——, *A Third Harvest of Souvenir Spoons*. 1968. Hardt.

Rainwater, D. T. and Felger, D. H., *American Spoons—Souvenir and Historical*. 1969. Thomas Nelson, Inc., Copewood & Davis Sts., Camden, N.J. 08101

GENERAL

A Dictionary of Marks, edited by Margaret Macdonald-Taylor, 1962. Hawthorn Books, Inc., 70 Fifth Ave., New York, N.Y. 10011

Antiques, Oddities, and Curiosities, Edward C. Warman. Warman Publishing Company, 8 Frank Hoover St., Uniontown, Pa. 15401

Antiques of the Future, James Mackay, 1970. Studio Vista. (London)

The Collecting Man, John Bedford, 1968. David McKay Company, 750 Third Ave., New York, N.Y. 10017

Gold in Your Attic, 1958. *More Gold in Your Attic,* 1961. Van Allen Bradley. Fleet Press Corporation, 156 Fifth Avenue, New York, N.Y. 10016

How to Collect the "New" Antiques, Ann Kilburn Cole, 1966. David McKay, 750 Third Avenue, New York, N.Y. 10017

Looking in Junk Shops and *More Looking in Junk Shops,* John Bedford, David McKay, 750 Third Avenue, New York, N.Y. 10017

Poor Man's Guide to Antique Collecting, John Mebane, 1971. Doubleday & Company, Garden City, N.Y. 11530

Treasure at Home, John Mebane, 1964. Barnes & Noble, 105 Fifth Avenue, New York, N.Y. 10003

Coca-Cola Collectibles, Shelly and Helen Goldstein. Shelly Goldstein, 5953 Ellenview Avenue, Woodland Hills, Calif. 91364

A History of Valentines, Ruth Webb Lee. Lee Publications, 105 Suffolk Road, Wellesley Hills, Mass. 02181

PUBLICATIONS

Antique Monthly
Tuscaloosa, Alabama 35401

Antique Trader Weekly
Dubuque, Iowa 52001

Antiques Journal
Dubuque, Iowa 52001

Apollo
Bracken House
10 Cannon Street
London, England

Art and Antiques Weekly
2 Arundel Street, WC2
London, England

Better Homes and Gardens
1716 Locust Street
Des Moines, Iowa 50303

Collectors' Den
151 Wonderland City
San Antonio, Texas 78201

Collector's Weekly
P. O. Box 1119
Kermit, Texas 79745

Connoisseur
224 West 57th Street
New York, New York 10019

Eastern Antiquity
Washington, New Jersey 07882

Gallery of California Antiques
3717 Mt. Diablo Blvd.
Lafayette, California 94549

Hobbies—THE MAGAZINE FOR COLLECTORS
1006 South Michigan Avenue
Chicago, Illinois 60605

House Beautiful
717 Fifth Avenue
New York, New York 10022

Joel Sater's *Antiques News*
Marietta, Pennsylvania 17547

Long John Latham's *Collector's World*
3201 North Frazier Street
Conroe, Texas 77301

New Yorker
25 West 43rd Street
New York, New York 10017

The Numismatist
P. O. Box 2366
Colorado Springs, Colorado 80901

Town & Country
717 Fifth Avenue
New York, New York 10022

Western Antique Mart
Eugene, Oregon 97402

Western Collector
511 Harrison Street
San Francisco, California 94105

Yankee Magazine
Dublin, New Hampshire 03444

MUSEUMS

Baltimore Museum of Art, Maryland
Bristol Clock Museum, Bristol, Connecticut
Boston Museum of Fine Arts, Massachusetts
Cincinnati Art Museum, Ohio
Cleveland Museum of Art, Ohio
Corning Glass Museum, Corning, New York
Detroit Institute of Arts, Michigan
Essex Institute, Salem, Massachusetts
Fogg Museum of Art, Boston, Massachusetts
Metropolitan Museum of Art, New York, New York
Museum of Modern Art, New York, New York
Musical Wonder House, Wiscasset, Maine
Philadelphia Museum of Art, Pennsylvania
Raggedy Ann Antique Doll and Toy Museum, Hobe, New Jersey
San Francisco Museum of Art, California
Smithsonian Institution, Washington, D.C.
Solomon R. Guggenheim Museum, New York, New York
Toledo Museum of Art, Ohio
West Point Museum, West Point, New York

ABROAD

British Museum, London, England
Dyson Perrins Museum, Worcester, England
The Louvre, Paris, France
National Gallery, London, England
Prado Museum, Madrid, Spain

Uffizi, Forence, Italy
Victoria and Albert Museum, London, England
Wallace Collection, London, England
Wedgwood Museum, Barlston, England

RESTORATIONS

Colonial Williamsburg, Williamsburg, Virginia
Old Sturbridge Village, Sturbridge, Massachusetts

DEALERS

(If you cannot locate the items you are seeking, this list of specialized dealers may prove helpful.)

AUTOGRAPHS

Bernard and Bruce Gimelson, Inc.
Fort Washington Industrial Park
Fort Washington, Pennsylvania 19034

Carnegie Book Shop
140 East 59th Street
New York, New York 10022

Charles Hamilton Autographs, Inc.
25 East 77th Street
New York, New York 10021

Goodspeed's Book Shop, Inc.
18 Beacon Street
Boston, Massachusetts 02108

Hostick, King V.
901 College Avenue
Springfield, Illinois 62704

Kronovet, Dr. Milton
75 Ocean Avenue
Brooklyn, New York 11225

Paul C. Richards
101 Monmouth Street
Brookline, Massachusetts 02146

Walter R. Benjamin Autographs, Inc.
790 Madison Avenue
New York, New York 10021

CHINA, GLASS, SILVER

Armstrong's
150 East Third Street
Pomona, California 91766

Baccarat Crystal
55 East 57th Street
New York, New York 10022

J. A. Buchroeder & Company, Inc.
1021 East Broadway
Columbia, Missouri 65201

Collectors International Limited
6 North Street
Mount Vernon, New York 10551

Craft House
Colonial Williamsburg
Williamsburg, Virginia 23185

Georg Jensen
601 Madison Avenue
New York, New York 10022

My Grandfather's Shop, Ltd.
8055 13th Street
Silver Spring, Maryland 20910

Steuben Glass
Fifth Avenue & 56th Street
New York, New York 10022

Tiffany & Company
Fifth Avenue & 57th Street
New York, New York 10022

DOLLS AND TOYS

F. A. O. Schwarz Children's World
745 Fifth Avenue
New York, New York 10022

Tudor House
P. O. Box 595
Scarsdale, New York

MUSIC BOXES

Hildegarde Studios
597 Farmington Avenue
Hartford, Connecticut 06105

The Merry Music Box
Todd Avenue
Boothbay Harbor, Maine 04538

Rita Ford, Inc.
812 Madison Avenue
New York, New York 10021

G. Schirmer, Inc.
4 East 49th Street
New York, New York 10017

PAPERWEIGHTS

Baccarat Crystal
55 East 57th Street
New York, New York 10022

Cristal d'Albret
Fine stores and shops
L. H. Selman Antiques
23 White Street
San Francisco, California 94109

Saks Fifth Avenue
Fifth Avenue & 49th Street
New York, New York 10022

Steuben Glass
Fifth Avenue & 56th Street
New York, New York 10022

Tiffany & Company
Fifth Avenue & 57th Street
New York, New York 10022

COLLECTORS' CLUBS AND SOCIETIES

AUTOGRAPHS

Universal Autograph Collectors Club
3109 Brighton, 7th Ave.
Brooklyn, New York 11235

BOTTLES

Avon Bottle Collectors Club
P. O. Box 8683
Detroit, Michigan 48224

Bud Hastin's National Avon Club
Kansas City, Missouri

Double Springs Collectors Club
13311 Illinois Avenue
Westminster, California 92683

Jim Beam Bottle & Specialty Club
490 El Camino, Real
Belmont, California 94002
(At least 40 affiliates around the country.)

International Avon Collectors Club
Mesa, Arizona 85201

Lionstone Bottle Collectors of America
Los Angeles, California

National Bottle & Collectables Club USA, Inc.
P. O. Box 65
Amador City, California 95601

National Grenadier Porcelain Bottle Club of America
Mullins, South Carolina 29574

CHINA

Wedgwood Collectors Society
801 Walnut Street
Philadelphia, Pennsylvania 19107

MEDALLIC ART

American Numismatic Association
818 North Cascade Avenue
Colorado Springs, Colorado

Franklin Mint Collectors Society
Franklin Center, Pennsylvania 19063

MUSIC BOXES

Musical Box Society Internationale
812 Madison Avenue
New York, New York 10021

PAPERWEIGHTS

Paperweight Collectors' Association
P. O. Box 128
Scarsdale, New York 10583

PLAYING CARDS

Chicago Playing Card Collectors, Inc.
9645 South Leavitt Street
Chicago, Illinois 60643

Playing Cards Collectors' Association, Inc.
Sturgeon Bay, Wisconsin 54235

CATALOGUES AND HOUSE ORGANS

Annual Bulletin of the Paperweight Collectors' Association
Scarsdale, New York 10583

Catalogue of Collectors Paperweights
23 White Street
San Francisco, California 94109

The Collector
Walter R. Benjamin Autographs, Inc.
790 Madison Avenue
New York, New York 10021

Collector's Guide
My Grandfather's Shop, Ltd.
8055 13th Street
Silver Spring, Maryland 20910

Collector's Newsletter
J. A. Buchroeder & Company
1021 East Broadway
Columbia, Missouri 65201

Craft House Catalogue
Colonial Williamsburg
Williamsburg, Virginia 23185

Franklin Mint Almanac
Franklin Mint
Franklin Center, Pennsylvania 19063

Newsletter
Wedgwood Collectors Society
801 Walnut Street
Philadelphia, Pennsylvania 19107

Numismatic Issues of The Franklin Mint
Franklin Center, Pennsylvania 19063

PRICE GUIDES

Antique Trader
Price Guide to Antiques and Collectors' Items
Babka Publishing Company
Dubuque, Iowa 52001

Antiques & Curios
HC Publishers, Inc.
220 Fifth Avenue
New York, New York 10001

Curios and Collectibles, A Price Guide to the New Antiques
Dafran House Publishers, Inc.
25 West 39th Street
New York, New York 10018

Hugh Cleveland's Bottle Pricing Guide
Cleveland Book Supply
320 Main Street
San Angelo, Texas 76901

Western Collector's Handbook and Price Guide to Avon Collectables
Western Collector Books
511 Harrison Street
San Francisco, California 94105

Western Collector Handbook and Price Guide to EZRA BROOKS
Western Collector Books
511 Harrison Street
San Francisco, California 94105

WHO'S WHO
A FEW OF THE WORLD'S
LEADING MANUFACTURERS
OF COLLECTIBLES

A. MICHELSEN
Copenhagen, Denmark
Famous Danish silversmiths founded in 1841 and selected by
the king of Denmark as "Insignia Jewelers" in 1846. Four generations of this family have headed this firm and Jorgen Michelsen
is now chairman of the board.

ARABIA
Helsinki, Finland
Well-known pottery founded in 1874 and named for a nine-
teenth-century villa whose owner was interested in Islamic art.

BACCARAT CRYSTAL
Baccarat, France
Fine glassware has been made from the early 1800s to the
present time. Especially noted for its exquisite paperweights.

BING & GRØNDAHL
Copenhagen, Denmark
This fine porcelain manufactory was founded in 1853 and the
originator of the Christmas plates.

GUSTAVSBERG
Stockholm, Sweden
Founded in the early 1800s, this Swedish porcelain manufactory

has successfully competed with the old established Scandinavian firms of Royal Copenhagen, Bing & Grøndahl and Rörstrand.

HAVILAND
Limoges, France
Founded in the mid-nineteenth century and still under the management of the famous Haviland family.

IMPERIAL GLASS
Bellaire, Ohio
Recognized since 1904 as manufacturer of fine handmade American glassware. Produce both blown and pressed glassware; also hand-cut, decorated and etched.

KASTRUP-HOLMEGAARD
Copenhagen, Denmark
The largest glass factory in Scandinavia and currently the only firm in Denmark engaged in the manufacture of household glassware. Holmegaard was founded in 1825 and Kastrup Glasvaerk in 1847 as a division of Holmegaard. It became independent in 1873, but in 1965 both firms were united again.

ORREFORS
Orrefors, Sweden
In 1726 this company was founded as an ironworks and its modest glass production began in 1898. After World War I, Orrefors developed new techniques such as graal glass and set new standards in the art of glassmaking.

PORSGRUND
Porsgrunn, Norway
In the mid-1800s this china manufactory came into existence under the helm of Jeremiason Johan, a shipowner, and has been a family operation ever since.

ROSENTHAL
Selb, Germany
Headed by Philip Rosenthal II, this renowned porcelain factory dates back to 1879 when his father, Philipp Rosenthal (two p's in Philip) was sent to Bavaria to buy china for an American firm and decided to become a manufacturer.

RÖRSTRAND
Stora Rörstrand, Sweden
This is Sweden's oldest porcelain manufactory, formed in 1726. Rörstrand is sold throughout the world. In the United States there are over 500 retail outlets.

ROYAL COPENHAGEN
Copenhagen, Denmark
Since 1779 the name "Royal Copenhagen" has epitomized the finest in dinnerware, objets d'art and figurines. Its sponsorship by the Crown was under the personal supervision of the Queen Dowager, Julianne Marie.

ROYAL CROWN DERBY
Derby, England
The oldest china manufactory in England (established 1750) and the only one entitled to mark its wares with both the words "Royal" and "Crown." Has supplied china to every monarch of England since the reign of George III and to other royalty and leading persons of the world.

ROYAL DOULTON
Burslem, England
The name Doulton in the world of porcelain and pottery dates back to John Doulton who in 1877 bought an established pottery in Burslem where the present manufactory is located.

ROYAL WORCESTER
Worcester, England
Founded in 1751 by Dr. John Wall, this is the only china company in Great Britain to have been in continuous production for over 200 years.

SPODE-COPELAND
Stoke, England
The company began with Josiah Spode (1773–97) who was descended from a long line of Staffordshire potters. Soon after his own pottery was established, William Copeland, a tea merchant, became his partner.

STEUBEN GLASS
Corning, New York
Traces its history to the turn of the century when Frederick Carder established a glass factory in Corning, New York (named after Steuben County in which the city of Corning is located). His factory was acquired in 1918 by Corning Glass Works and became the Steuben Division of the company. Since 1933 Steuben Glass has been headed by Arthur Amory Houghton, Jr., great-grandson of the founder of Corning Glass Works.

UNITED STATES PLAYING CARD COMPANY
Cincinnati, Ohio
Founded in 1894, this company was an outgrowth of the United

States Printing Company, which was formed from the nucleus of Russell, Morgan and Company. Their antecedents go back to the Cincinnati *Enquirer* Job Printing Department which produced circus, theatrical posters and playing cards.

VAL ST. LAMBERT
Belgium
Creators of fine crystal since 1840.

WATERFORD GLASS
Ireland
Established in 1729. One of the most well-known glassmakers in the world.

WEDGWOOD
Stoke-on-Trent, England
Established 1759. Introduced Cream Ware in 1761, Black Basalt 1766 and Jasper 1775.

VALUATIONS—A SELECTED LISTING

Prices will vary from time to time in the same manner as those on the commodity markets. The important determining factors are (1) supply and demand (2) rarity of the piece and (3) desirability and condition of the item.

As this book goes to press, these are the latest asking quotations we have seen either in catalogues, magazines, newspapers and price guides or listed with manufacturers, dealers and collectors.

JIM BEAM BOTTLES	1971 Prices
Political Series	
1964 Elephant and Donkey Boxers	$ 31.00
1968 Elephant and Donkey Clowns	15.00
1970 Agnew	3,000.00
Club Bottles	
1967 Blue Fox	193.50
1968 Yuma Rifle Club	39.45
1969 Gold Fox	92.30
1970 California Mission	32.50

Executive Series

1955	Royal Porcelain	181.05
1956	Royal Gold Round	149.60
1957	Royal Di Monte	76.60
1958	Grey Cherub	142.90
1959	Tavern Scene	70.25
1960	Blue Cherub	82.95
1961	Golden Chalice	72.90
1962	Flower Basket	50.75
1963	Royal Rose	51.50
1964	Royal Gold Diamond	47.25
1965	Marbled Fantasy	79.65
1966	Majestic	37.50
1967	Prestige	21.30
1968	Presidential	12.10
1969	Sovereign	12.55
1970	Charisma	14.45

Centennial Series

1960	Santa Fe	199.10
1961	Civil War	40.05
1964	St. Louis	25.90
1966	Alaska Purchase	23.35
1967	Cheyenne	14.10
1968	Reno	6.65
1969	Baseball	6.45
1970	Preakness	8.10

Trophy Series

1957	Duck	40.98
1958	Ram	114.65
1961	Pheasant	18.80
1962	Horses	22.25
1963	Doe	34.40
1965	Fox	46.25
1966	Eagle	15.55
1967	Cats	11.50
1968	Cardinal	39.70
1969	Blue Jay	8.60
1970	Poodle	9.25

State Series

1958	Alaska	82.10
1959	Hawaii	72.95
1960	Kansas	69.10

1963 West Virginia	125.50
1964 North Dakota	83.00
1965 Wyoming	72.45
1966 Ohio	16.20
1967 Kentucky	15.80
1967 Nebraska	12.85
1968 Illinois	8.40
1969 South Dakota Mount Rushmore	7.50
1970 Maine	10.70

Customer's Specialties

1956 Foremost Pink-Speckled Beauty	280.00
1957 Harold's Club Silver Opal	20.00
1957 Man in Barrel No. 1	390.70
1958 Man in Barrel No. 2	287.75
1962 Marina City	43.60
1963 Harrahs Club	539.00
1964 1st National Bank of Chicago	2,163.00
1965 Pinwheel	86.45

EZRA BROOKS

Collector's Series

Potbellied Stove	8.30
Golden Antique Cannon	8.20
Jack of Diamonds	8.80
Overland Express Stagecoach	8.95
Iron Horse Train	8.20
Flintlock Dueling Pistol	8.20
Cigar Store Indian	8.00
Gun Series (Set of 4)	18.30
Gold Miner	10.55
Cheyenne	11.90
Club Bottle	117.50

Commemorative Series

Winston Churchill	8.25
Silver Dollar	14.90
Liberty Bell	10.65
Man of War	12.15
Ticker Tape	9.85
Go Big Red	36.85

City and State

San Francisco Cable Car	7.70
Wichita Centennial	21.05

New Hampshire   24.10
Indy Racer   19.85
Ontario "500" Racer   12.35
West Virginia Mountaineer   26.25

Customer's Specialties
Zimmerman's Old Hat   17.25
Katz Cats   13.45
Golden Rooster   142.50
Big Daddy   15.95
Bucket of Blood   28.55
Foremost Astronaut   14.70
Golden Horseshoe   64.10
Border Town Club   21.85
Big Bertha   24.60
Nugget Classic   26.45

FAMOUS FIRSTS

1968 Marmon Wasp   21.50
1969 Renault Racer   24.50
1970 Large Yacht America   75.00
1971 Robert E. Lee   24.50

GRENADIER SOLDIERS

1969 Napoleon   18.95
1969 Lassal   12.95
1969 Ney   12.95
1969 Eugène   12.95
1969 Lannes   12.95
1969 Murat   12.95
1969 2nd Maryland 1777   18.95
1969 Continental Marines 1779   12.95
1969 Baylors 3rd Continental 1778   12.95
1969 3rd New York 1779   12.95
1969 1st Pennsylvania 1775   18.95
1969 18th Continental 1778   12.95
1970 First Officer's Guard 1804   12.95
1970 Dragoon 17th Regiment 1812   12.95

LIONSTONE BOTTLES

1969 Gentleman Gambler   15.75
1970 Gold Panner   22.10

1970	Bartender	28.75
1970	Highway Robber	22.65
1970	Squaw Man	22.60
1970	Wells Fargo Guard	17.65
1970	Vigilante	17.65
1970	Mountain Man	22.60
1970	Stagecoach Driver	22.70
1970	Frontiersman	22.60
1970	Sodbuster	18.60
1970	Railroad Engineer	18.50
1970	Circuit Riding Judge	18.70
1970	Jesse James	18.75
1970	Riverboat Captain	18.25
1970	Gambel Quail	32.95

STEUBEN GLASS

The Great Koala	
Lloyd Atkins	700.00
Duckling	
Lloyd Atkins	130.00
Trout and Fly	
James Houston	675.00
Eagle, James Houston	225.00
Cat	170.00
Porpoise, Lloyd	
Atkins	85.00
Snail	45.00

FRANKLIN MINT

		Net Mint Final	Metal	Issue Price	Price Guide
Apollo XI Commemorative	1969	2,281	Silver	6.00	28.00
Apollo Project Memorial	1967	511	Silver	10.00	20.00
Apollo 8 Moon Flight	1969	5,252	Silver	7.25	22.00
Apollo XI Moon Landing	1969	5,252	Silver	7.25	28.00
Apollo XV Moon Landing	1971		Silver	10.00	

	Net Mint Final	Metal	Issue Price	Price Guide
Coins of Tunisia (Ten Coins)	1969　15,202	Silver	77.00	135.00
Fine Art Plaques				
John F. Kennedy by Gilroy Roberts	1967　50	Silver	750.00	1,800.00
Wild Geese by Gilroy Roberts	1969　50	Silver	750.00	1,450.00
Toreador and Bull by Umberto Romano	1969　225	Silver	250.00	550.00
Children at Play by Charles Parks	1969　200	Silver	375.00	700.00

PORCELAIN AND POTTERY

CHRISTMAS PLATES　*1971 Price*

Anri
1971　Alpine Scene (1st Issue)　45.00

Bareuther
1967　(1st Issue) Stifskirche　65.00
1968　Kappelkirche　15.00
1969　Christkindlemarkt　13.00
1970　Chapel in Oberndorf　12.50
1971　12.00

Bing & Grøndahl

1895	1,875.00	1950–56	100.00
1896	1,275.00	1957	125.00
1897	825.00	1958	100.00
1898	450.00	1959	125.00
1899	750.00	1960	110.00
1900	500.00	1961	85.00
1901–03	250.00	1962	60.00
1904–11	85.00	1963–65	75.00
1912–19	75.00	1966	60.00
1920–33	70.00	1967	50.00
1934–37	75.00	1968	40.00
1938–44	150.00	1969	30.00
1945	200.00	1970	30.00
1946–49	100.00	1971	15.00

Haviland

1970	Partridge in a Pear Tree (1st Issue)	35.00
1971	Two Turtle Doves	25.00

Hummel

1971	Annual by W. Goebel	25.00

Imperial

1970	Partridge in a Pear Tree (1st Issue)	17.50
1971	Two Turtle Doves	16.50

Porsgrund

1968	Church Scene (1st Issue)	35.00
1969	Three Kings	11.00
1970	Road to Bethlehem	9.00
1971	A Child Is Born	8.00

Rörstrand

1968	Bringing Home the Tree	100.00
1969	Jul	12.00
1970	Nils with his Geese	11.00
1971	Nils in Lapland	10.00

Rosenthal

1910–1955	(some years not available)	45.00
1956–1968		45.00
1969–1970		45.00
1971		42.00

Royal Copenhagen

1908	1,200.00	1951	350.00
1909–10	150.00	1952–54	100.00
1911–18	100.00	1955	180.00
1919–33	100.00	1956	140.00
1934–35	125.00	1957–59	150.00
1936–37	140.00	1960–61	100.00
1938–39	225.00	1962	160.00
1940–42	420.00	1963–64	100.00
1943	500.00	1965–66	60.00
1944	230.00	1967	60.00
1945	350.00	1968	50.00
1946	200.00	1969	30.00
1947	230.00	1970	30.00
1948–50	175.00	1971	15.00

Royale
1969   35.00
1970   15.00
1971   13.00

Spode
1970   Christmas Plate—A Partridge in
      a Pear Tree   35.00
1971   Christmas Plate—Ding, Dong,
      Merrily on High   35.00

Svend Jensen
1970   Hans Christian Andersen's House   16.00
1971   The Little Match Girl   15.00

Wedgwood
1969   (1st Issue)   79.50
1970   Trafalgar Square   25.00
1971   30.00

Franklin Mint
1971   Norman Rockwell
      Christmas Plate   500.00
      (originally 100.00)
1971   Christmas Ingot   12.00

MOTHER'S DAY PLATES   *1971 Prices*

Bareuther
1969   Mother and Children (1st Issue)   50.00
1970   Mother and Children   12.50
1971   Mother and Children   12.00

Bing & Grøndahl
1969   Dog and Puppies (1st Issue)   175.00
1970   Bird and Chicks   22.50
1971   Cat and Kittens   12.00

Lund & Clausen
1970   Rose (1st issue)   15.00
1971   Forget-me-nots   12.50

Porsgrund
1970   Mare and Foal (1st issue)   15.00
1971   Boy and Geese   7.50

Royal Copenhagen
1971 (1st issue)   70.00

Svend Jensen
1970 A Bouquet for Mother (1st issue)   15.00
1971 Mother's Love   15.00

Wedgwood
1971 (1st issue)   20.00

BURGUES

Limited Editions	*1971 Prices*	*Edition Limited to*
American Goldfinches with Morning Glories	1,250.00	150
White-throated Sparrow	800.00	250
Junco on Snow	600.00	250
Belted Kingfisher Fledgling	350.00	750
Ruby-throated Hummingbird	600.00	300
Golden-winged Warbler in Nest	1,100.00	100
Owl	450.00	500
Veiltail Goldfish Decorated	875.00	150
White-breasted Nuthatches	3,500.00	75
Cave Swallows, male and female	750.00	500
King Penguin Group	850.00	350
Golden-crowned Kinglet	500.00	450
Red-breasted Nuthatch	225.00	950
Chipmunk with Acorns	150.00	750
Fledgling Bluejay	125.00	non-limited

EDWARD MARSHALL BOEHM

Fledglings (baby birds)
Cedar Waxwing	65.00
Robin	75.00
Eastern Bluebird	75.00
Wood Thrush	80.00
Goldfinch	75.00
Crested Flycatcher	80.00
Chickadee	65.00
Magpie	75.00
Blackburnian Warbler	70.00
Western Bluebirds	125.00
Red Poll	75.00

Non-Limited

Canada Geese, pr.	500.00
White-throated sparrow	250.00
Yellow-throated warbler	325.00
Black-capped Chickadee	225.00
Hummingbird	325.00
Nuthatch	225.00
E. M. Boehm Orchid	350.00
La Pietà Madonna	150.00

CYBIS PORCELAINS

Limited Editions	*1971 Prices*	*Edition Limited to*
Blue-gray Gnatcatchers	2,500.00	200 pr.
Skylarks	1,850.00	350 pr.
Solitary Sandpipers	1,500.00	400 pr.
Wood duck	400.00	500
American Screech Owl with Virginia Creeper	1,500.00	500
Christmas Rose	450.00	500
Calla Lily	850.00	500
Narcissus	425.00	500
Clematis with House Wren	1,300.00	500
Dutch Crocus, Blue Enchantress or Golden Goblet, 8½″×10″	550.00	700
Unicorn	1,250.00	500
Nashua, 16″×20″ with Vitrine	2,000.00	500
Eleanor of Aquitaine, 13″ with Vitrine	875.00	750
Juliet	2,000.00	800
Tranquility Base, Apollo 11 Commemorative	1,500.00	111

North American Indian Series		
Onondaga, "Hiawatha"	1,500.00	500
Dakota, "Laughing Water," Minnehaha	1,500.00	500
Blackfeet, "Beaverhead," Medicine Man	2,000.00	500

Non-Limited Woodland Collection	
Baby Owl 4½″ color	30.00
Wood Wren with Dogwood	135.00
Duckling, Baby Brother	50.00
Mushroom, Jack-O'-Lantern	225.00
Snail, "Sir Henri Escargot"	135.00

Magnolia	175.00	
Windflower	95.00	
Enchanted Prince, American Bullfrog	250.00	

Storybook Characters

First Flight	40.00
Heidi	125.00
Wendy	50.00
Thumbelina	45.00
Rebecca	110.00
Pandora	75.00

Animals

Burro, "Fitzgerald"	50.00
Buffalo	45.00
Colts, "Darby & Joan"	250.00
Madonna, "Queen of Angels"	90.00
Madonna with bird	150.00

ISPANKY

Limited Edition

On the Trail	675.00	350
The Hunt	1,200.00	350
Calvary Scout	675.00	350
Pack Horse	500.00	350
Forty-Niner	200.00	550
Drummer Boy	800.00	120
Pioneer Woman	150.00	350
Pilgrim Family	350.00	550
King Arthur	225.00	500
Ballet Dancers	200.00	500
Ballerina	225.00	500
Love	250.00	300
Rosh Hashana	275.00	400
Moses	350.00	400
Storm	385.00	500
Horse	250.00	300
Owl	600.00	300
Tulips	1,800.00	250
Orchids	1,000.00	250
Birds of Paradise	1,400.00	250
Daffodils	800.00	250
Romeo and Juliet	275.00	500

Pegasus	285.00	300
Meditation	250.00	300

Unlimited Edition

Alice in Wonderland	90.00
Huck Finn	100.00
Peter Pan	100.00
Pied Piper	75.00
Heidi	110.00
Mandolin Player	75.00
Elizabeth	120.00

ROYAL COPENHAGEN

Henrik and Else	375.00
Goose Girl	75.00
The Gossips	250.00
Knitting Woman	120.00
Whittling Boy	80.00
Boy with Teddy Bear	85.00
Amager Girl	360.00
White Duck	29.00
Lioness	118.00
Siamese Cat	49.00
Rooster	56.00
Love Birds	53.00
Baby Robin	16.50
Owls	35.00
Woman with Goats	180.00
Two Ducks	69.00
Mouse on Sugar	20.00
Little Mermaid	250.00
White Cock	21.00

ROYAL WORCESTER

Collector's Miniatures

Onion vase	16.50
Raised trinket box	19.50
Petite trinket box	16.50
Tricornered trinket box	23.50
Boutique bottle	16.50
Heart tray	15.00
Oval cache box	22.50
Sachet vase	22.50

Clover box	25.00
Facet box	25.00
Midas box	27.50

Bisque Chinoiserie Figurines by A. Azori

L'Oiseau	79.50
La Fleur	79.50
Le Miroir	79.50
Le Panier	79.50

Tropical Fish by Ronald Van Ruyckevelt

Four-eyed Fish	36.00
Blue Angel Fish	42.50
Yellow Grunt	52.50
Spadefish	42.50
Red Hind	52.50
Sergeant Major	36.00

Days of the Week Figurines by Freda Doughty

Sunday's Child (girl)	47.50
Sunday's Child (boy)	38.50
Monday's Child (girl)	36.50
Monday's Child (boy)	47.50
Tuesday's Child (girl)	49.50
Tuesday's Child (boy)	49.50
Wednesday's Child (girl)	42.50
Wednesday's Child (boy)	42.50
Thursday's Child (girl)	49.50
Thursday's Child (boy)	42.50
Friday's Child (girl)	42.50
Friday's Child (boy)	42.50
Saturday's Child (girl)	39.50
Saturday's Child (boy)	57.50

Months of the Year Figurines by Freda Doughty

January	49.50
February	42.50
March	49.50
April	69.50
May	45.00
June	49.50
July	57.50
August	49.50
September	49.50
October	57.50
November	72.50

December	49.50

Children by Freda Doughty

Grandmother's Dress, blue, pink or yellow	42.50
Parakeet Boy, blue, pink or yellow	55.00
Sweet Anne, shaded green	38.00
First Dance, green	57.50
Only Me	25.00
Polly Put the Kettle On	32.50
Nun	12.50
Monk	12.50

Bird Series by Dorothy Doughty

Year of Issue	Price	Edition	Quantity Completed
1968 Redstarts	2,100.00 pr.	500 prs.	280 prs.
1965 Kingfisher	1,500.00	500	293
1965 Chiffchaff	1,800.00	500	422
1964 Blue-Tits	1,500.00 pr.	500 prs.	330 prs.
1968 Gray Wagtail	750.00	500	270
1964 Wrens	1,500.00 pr.	500 prs.	389 prs.
1964 Robin	–	500	498
1964 Lesser Whitethroats	–	500 prs.	490 prs.
1970 Moorhen Chick	1,000.00	500	73

Equestrian Series by Doris Lindner

Year of Issue	Price	Edition	Quantity Completed
1947 H.M. The Queen	–	100	100
1959 The Winner	700.00	Unlimited	–
1960 Foxhunter	700.00	500	413
1961 Officer of the Life Guards	850.00	150	147
1961 Officer of the Royal Horse Guards	850.00	150	127
1962 Quarterhorse	500.00	500	337
1963 Merano	750.00	500	193
1963 Arab Stallion	–	500	500
1964 Shire Stallion	800.00	500	283
1965 Hyperion	600.00	500	417
1966 Percheron	800.00	500	212
1966 Welsh Mountain Pony	550.00	500	496
1966 Royal Canadian Mounted Policeman	1,000.00	500	491
1967 Arkle	–	500	500

Year of Issue	Price	Edition	Quantity Completed
1968 H.R.H. The Duke of Edinburgh	1,300.00	750	461
1969 Appaloosa	650.00	750	232
1969 Suffolk Punch	750.00	500	87
1970 Marion Coakes-Mould	750.00	750	22

Prize Cattle Series by Doris Lindner

1959 Hereford Bull	450.00	1,000	665
1961 Jersey Cow	400.00	500	312
1961 Aberdeen Angus Bull	450.00	500	448
1961 Santa Gertrudis Bull	450.00	500	267
1964 British Friesian Bull	550.00	500	228
1964 Jersey Bull	550.00	500	138
1966 Dairy Shorthorn Bull	600.00	500	137
1968 Brahman Bull	550.00	500	189
1968 Charolais Bull	550.00	500	227

Equestrian Series by Doris Lindner (Unlimited Editions)

1936 Hog Hunting	450.00
1936 Huntsman and Hounds	450.00
1936 At the Meet	350.00
1936 Cantering to the Post	350.00
1936 Over the Sticks	350.00
1936 Polo Player	400.00
1950 Two Galloping Horses	900.00
1936 Three Circus Horses Rearing	1,650.00
1936 In the Ring	1,650.00

Tropical Fish Series by Ronald Van Ruyckevelt

1958 Red Hind	450.00	500	422
1956 Spanish Hogfish and Sergeant Major	450.00	500	426
1957 Four-Eyed and Banded Butterfly Fish	450.00	500	411
1958 Blue Angel Fish	450.00	500	332
1961 Squirrel Fish	525.00	500	341
1964 Rock Beauty	500.00	500	308
1968 Rainbow Parrot Fish	500.00	500	–

Year of Issue	Price	Edition	Quantity Completed
Game Fish Series by Ronald Van Ruyckevelt			
1962 Sailfish	500.00	500	328
1962 Flying Fish	525.00	500	211
1964 Tarpon	600.00	500	212
1965 Blue Marlin	600.00	500	222
1968 Dolphin	600.00	500	118
Tropical Flower Series by Ronald Van Ruyckevelt			
1961 Passion Flower	625.00	500	394
1962 Hibiscus	625.00	500	242
American Game Birds Series by Ronald Van Ruyckevelt			
1968 Ring-Necked Pheasants	2,500.00 pr.	500 prs.	260 prs.
1968 Mallards	2,500.00 pr.	500 prs.	311 prs.
1969 Bob White Quail	1,500.00 pr.	500 prs.	143 prs.
1970 American Pintail	2,500.00 pr.	500 prs.	87 prs.
Victorian Figures Series by Ruth Van Ruyckevelt			
1959 Penelope	–	500	500
1959 Lisette	–	500	500
1960 Beatrice	–	500	500
1960 Caroline		500	500
1962 Rebecca	600.00	500	470
1962 Louisa	600.00	500	478
1964 The Tea Party	1,500.00	250	246
1964 Rosalind	300.00	500	498
1964 Melanie	300.00	500	498
1968 Charlotte and Jane	1,300.00	500	109
1967 Elizabeth	500.00	500	468
1967 Madelaine	500.00	500	469
1968 Marion	400.00	500	331
1969 Emily	400.00	500	241
1969 Bridget	400.00	500	245
Nursing Sisters Series by Ruth Van Ruyckevelt			
1963 Sister of the London Hospital	325.00	500	166
1963 Sister of the Nightingale Training School, St. Thomas Hospital	325.00	500	168

Year of Issue	Price	Edition	Quantity Completed
1966 Sister of the University College Hospital	325.00	500	80
1970 Sister of the Red Cross	350.00	750	49

Historical Figures Series by Frederick Gertner

1916 Henry VIII	550.00	Unlimited	–
1916 Mary Queen of Scots	400.00	Unlimited	–
1916 Edward VI	350.00	Unlimited	–
1917 Anne Boleyn	275.00	Unlimited	–
1917 Queen Elizabeth	650.00	Unlimited	–
1917 Sir Walter Raleigh	400.00	Unlimited	–
1917 Charles I	400.00	Unlimited	–
1917 Charles II	325.00	Unlimited	–

Military Figures Series by Frederick Gertner

1917 Officer of the 3rd Dragoon Guards	325.00	Unlimited	–
1917 Officer of the 17th Dragoon Guards, Circa 1814	350.00	Unlimited	–
1917 Admiral, Circa 1780	400.00	Unlimited	–
1917 Artillery Officer, Circa 1815	350.00	Unlimited	–
1917 Officer of the Seaforth Highlanders, Circa 1815	400.00	Unlimited	–
1917 Officer of the Coldstream Guards, Circa 1815	300.00	Unlimited	–
1954 Officer of the 29th Foot, the Worcestershire Regiment, Circa 1812	350.00	Unlimited	–

Papal Figures Series by Frederick Gertner & Neal French

1956 Trooper of the Papal Swiss Guard	700.00	150	77
1959 Privy Chamberlain of the Sword and Cape	700.00	150	68
1963 Colonel of the Noble Guard	850.00	150	46

Year of Issue	Price	Edition	Quantity Completed
1965 Officer of the Palatine Guard	700.00	150	36
1967 Papal Gendarme	650.00	150	12

Military Commanders Series by Bernard Winskill

1969 Napoleon Bonaparte	2,250.00	750	92
1970 Duke of Wellington	3,000.00	750	–

Ormolu Flowers by Ronald Van Ruyckevelt

1968 Mennecy A-101	600.00	500	215
1968 Mennacy A-102	600.00	500	215
1968 Honfleur A-105	500.00	500	197
1968 Honfleur A-106	500.00	500	195
1969 Argenteuil A-108	850.00	500	167
1969 St. Denis A-109	850.00	500	114
1969 Castelneau A-110	750.00	500	185

Index